ACE YOUR PHYSICS SCIENCE PROJECT

ACE YOUR SPORTS SCIENCE PROJECT

GREAT SCIENCE FAIR IDEAS

Madeline Goodstein,
Robert Gardner,
and
Barbara Gardner Conklin

Enslow Publishers, Inc.
40 Industrial Road
Box 398
Berkeley Heights, NJ 07922
USA

http://www.enslow.com

Library of Congress Cataloging-in-Publication Data

Goodstein, Madeline P.
    Ace your sports science project : great science fair ideas / Madeline Goodstein, Robert Gardner, and Barbara Gardner Conklin.
        p. cm. — (Ace your physics science project)
    Summary: "Presents several science experiments and project ideas dealing with the physics of sports"—Provided by publisher.
    Includes bibliographical references and index.
    ISBN-13: 978-0-7660-3229-3
    ISBN-10: 0-7660-3229-9
    1. Physics projects—Juvenile literature. 2. Physics—Juvenile literature. 3. Sports—Juvenile literature. 4. Physical education and training—Juvenile literature. I. Gardner, Robert, 1929– II. Conklin, Barbara Gardner. III. Title.
    QC33.G66 2009
    507.8—dc22

                                    2008004689

Printed in the United States of America

10 9 8 7 6 5 4 3 2 1

To Our Readers: We have done our best to make sure all Internet Addresses in this book were active and appropriate when we went to press. However, the author and the publisher have no control over and assume no liability for the material available on those Internet sites or on other Web sites they may link to. Any comments or suggestions can be sent by e-mail to comments@enslow.com or to the address on the back cover.

♻ Enslow Publishers, Inc., is committed to printing our books on recycled paper. The paper in every book contains 10% to 30% post-consumer waste (PCW). The cover board on the outside of each book contains 100% PCW. Our goal is to do our part to help young people and the environment too!

The experiments in this book are a collection of the authors' best experiments, which were previously published by Enslow Publishers, Inc. in *Health Science Projects About Sports Performance*, *Science Projects About the Physics of Sports*, and *Sports Science Projects: The Physics of Balls in Motion*.

Illustration Credits: Stephen F. Delisle

Photo Credits: © bubaone/iStockphoto.com, trophy icons; © Chen Fu Soh/iStockphoto.com, backgrounds; © Galina Barskaya/iStockphoto.com, p. 80; © Graffisimo/iStockphoto.com, p. 54; Shutterstock, pp. 1, 10, 96.

Cover Photos: Shutterstock

CONTENTS

CHAPTER 1

Physical Conditioning: Are You Ready for Action? 11

CHAPTER 2

What Makes a Good Athlete? 31

CHAPTER 3

Sports and Physics 55

⊙ **Indicates experiments that offer ideas for science fair projects.**

◔ *Indicates experiments that offer ideas for science fair projects.*

INTRODUCTION

When you hear the word *science*, do you think of a person in a white lab coat surrounded by beakers of bubbling liquids, specialized lab equipment, and computers? What exactly is science? Maybe you think science is only a subject you learn in school. Science is much more than that.

Science is the study of the things that are all around you, every day. No matter where you are or what you are doing, scientific principles are at work. You don't need special materials or equipment or even a white lab coat to be a scientist. Materials commonly found in your home, at school, or at a local store will allow you to become a scientist and pursue an area of interest. Even your sports equipment can help you learn science. By making careful observations and asking questions about how things work, you can begin to design experiments to investigate a variety of questions. You can do science. You probably already have but just didn't know it!

Perhaps you are reading this book because you are looking for an idea for a science fair project for school and you are interested in sports. Maybe you want to learn to play a new sport or become better at a sport you already play. This book will provide an opportunity for you to learn about a variety of sports. It will also teach you about how to stretch, warm up, and get in shape. There is a lot to know about exercise, fitness, and training. A good place to start is to test your physical condition, balance, flexibility, strength, and endurance. You can do this in Chapter 1. The rest of the chapters include experiments about baseball, basketball, football, golf, hockey, soccer, and tennis. Learning about the science behind catching, kicking, hitting, or shooting can help you improve your skills. Whether you play sports yourself or simply enjoy being a spectator, there is sure to be something to catch your interest. You will learn scientific principles that will help you increase your understanding of and interest in sports.

THE SCIENTIFIC METHOD

All scientists look at the world and try to understand how things work. They make careful observations and conduct research about a question. Different areas of science use different approaches. Depending on the phenomenon being investigated, one method is likely to be more appropriate than another. Designing a new medication for heart disease, studying the spread of an invasive plant species such as purple loosestrife, and finding evidence that there was once water on Mars all require different methods.

Despite the differences, however, all scientists use a similar general approach to do experiments. It is called the scientific method. In most experiments, some or all of the following steps are used: making observations, formulating a question, making a hypothesis (an answer to the question) and a prediction (an if-then statement), designing and conducting an experiment, analyzing results and drawing conclusions, and accepting or rejecting the hypothesis. Scientists then share their findings with others by writing articles that are published in journals. After—and only after—a hypothesis has repeatedly been supported by experiments can it be considered a theory.

You might be wondering how to get an experiment started. When you observe something in the world, you may become curious and come up with a question. Your question can be answered by a well-designed investigation. Your question may also arise from an earlier experiment or from background reading. Once you have a question, you should make a hypothesis. Your hypothesis is a possible answer to the question (what you think will happen). Once you have a hypothesis, it is time to design an experiment.

In some cases, it is appropriate to do a controlled experiment. This means there are two groups treated exactly the same except for the single factor that you are testing. That factor is often called a variable. For example, if you want to investigate whether exercise affects heart rate, two groups may be used. One group is called the control group, and the other is called the experimental group. The two groups of people should be treated exactly the same. The people in the control group will sit quietly for five minutes while the people in the experimental group will jog in place for five minutes. The variable is exercise—it is the thing that changes, and it is the only difference between the two groups.

During the experiment, you will collect data. For example, you will measure heart rate after the period of five minutes of either rest or exercise. You might also record the breathing rate for each person and the color of each person's face. By comparing the data collected from the control group with the data collected from the experimental group, you will draw conclusions. Since the two groups were treated exactly alike except for exercising, an increase in heart rate of the people in the experimental group would allow you to conclude with confidence that increased heart rate is a result of the one thing that was different: exercise.

Two other terms that are often used in scientific experiments are *dependent* and *independent* variables. The dependent variable here is heart rate, because it is the one you measure as an outcome. It may depend upon exercise. Exercise is the independent variable. It is the thing that the experimenter intentionally changes. After the data is collected, it is analyzed to see whether the hypothesis was supported or rejected. Often, the results of one experiment will lead you to a related question, or they may send you off in a different direction. Whatever the results, there is something to be learned from all scientific experiments.

SCIENCE FAIR PROJECT IDEAS

Many of the experiments in this book may be appropriate for science fair projects. Experiments marked with a symbol (⬇) include a section called Science Fair Project Ideas. The ideas in this section provide suggestions to help you develop your own original science fair project. However, judges at such fairs do not reward projects or experiments that are simply copied from a book. For example, a model of the layers of a baseball would probably not impress judges unless it was done in a novel or creative way. On the other hand, a carefully performed experiment to find out whether the angle at which a baseball is thrown affects the time it takes to reach home plate would probably receive careful consideration.

SCIENCE FAIRS

Science fair judges tend to reward creative thought and imagination. However, it is difficult to be creative or imaginative unless you are really interested in your project. If you decide to do a project, be sure to choose a topic that appeals to you. Consider, too, your own ability and the cost of materials. Don't pursue a project that you can't afford.

If you decide to use a project found in this book for a science fair, you will need to find ways to modify or extend it. That should not be difficult because you will probably find that as you do these projects new ideas for experiments will come to mind. These new experiments could make excellent science fair projects, particularly because they spring from your own mind and are interesting to you.

If you decide to enter a science fair and have never done so before, you should read some of the books listed in the Further Reading section. The books that deal specifically with science fairs will provide plenty of helpful hints and lots of useful information that will enable you to avoid the pitfalls that sometimes plague first-time entrants. You will learn how to prepare appealing reports that include charts and graphs, how to set up and display your work, how to present your project, and how to relate to judges and visitors.

SAFETY FIRST

As with many activities, safety is important in science and certain rules apply when conducting experiments. Some of the rules below may seem obvious to you, while others may not, but each is important to follow.

1. Have **an adult** help you whenever the book advises.

2. Wear eye protection and closed-toe shoes (rather than sandals) and tie back long hair.

3. Don't eat or drink while doing experiments and never taste substances being used.

4. Do only those experiments that are described in the book or those that have been approved by **an adult**.

5. Never engage in horseplay or play practical jokes.

6. Read through the entire experimental procedure to make sure you understand all instructions. Clear extra items from your work space.

7. At the end of every activity, clean all materials and put them away. Wash your hands thoroughly with soap and water.

Chapter 1

Physical Conditioning: Are You Ready for Action?

BEFORE PARTICIPATING IN PHYSICAL ACTIVITY YOU SHOULD PREPARE YOUR BODY FOR ACTION. A warm-up provides the body with a period of adjustment between rest and physical activity. Warming up increases the heart rate and the internal body temperature. The increased blood supply to the muscles and the higher internal temperature help to loosen the muscles, making them more pliable, relaxed, and less subject to injury.

Many athletic injuries are related to poor flexibility. Flexibility is determined by the elasticity of the connective tissue around the joints. Strenuous exercise can increase muscle tightness and reduce flexibility. Stretching before and after exercising will increase flexibility and help to prevent injuries, stiffness, or pain following exercise. There is some controversy as to whether to stretch before or after exercise. Most experts recommend stretching both before and after any intense physical activity.

Before you do any stretching, you need to increase blood flow to your muscles. You can do this by means of a warm-up activity, such as marching, brisk walking, or light jogging. You should warm up for at least five minutes. After the warm-up, stretch your muscles, concentrating on the ones you are going to use most during the physical activity. For example, if you are going to run, you should focus on your legs and feet.

Just a few stretches of all major muscles will prepare your body for any action and help with flexibility.

When you do a stretch, never bounce. Bouncing can cause a muscle to contract at the same time it is being stretched, which will reduce the effectiveness of the stretch and possibly cause muscle soreness. Instead, move gently into the stretch and then hold the position. Breathe naturally as you stretch. Do not hold your breath.

After you have completed your physical activity, you need to cool your body to prevent injury and muscle soreness. A cooldown is done in much the same way as the warm-up. Slow your activity to light jogging or brisk walking until your breathing and heart rate are no longer elevated. Then stretch your muscles again.

If the exercise you plan to do requires considerable use of certain parts of the body, you should do additional stretches to those areas before and afterward.

After you have warmed up, do the following stretches in the order presented. When you are finished exercising and cooling down, do the same stretches. Repeat each stretch a few times.

STRETCHING HEAD AND NECK

- Standing straight with knees slightly bent, lower your right ear toward your right shoulder, then raise your head to look forward. Do not roll your head back to look upward because this puts stress on the cervical vertebrae at the top of your spine. Lower your chin to your chest, then raise it. Do the same stretch for the left side.

- Turn your head to look over your right shoulder, then your left.

- Rotate your head in half circles to the right and to the left.

STRETCHING SHOULDERS AND ARMS

- Put your right forearm behind your head, as if you are trying to reach a zipper. Grab your right elbow with your left hand and gently pull the elbow behind your head until you feel slight tension in your right arm. Hold for a few seconds. Repeat on the other arm.

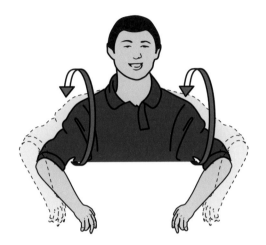

Stretching the arms and shoulders

- Put one arm across your chest at shoulder height. With your other hand, push the arm at the elbow into your body and hold. Repeat with the opposite arm.

- Slowly roll your shoulder joints in circles, both forward and backward. Then do circles with elbows bent and upper arms circling with the shoulders (see Figure 1a). Finally do full, slow vertical circles with your arms (see Figure 1b).

STRETCHING WAIST

- Standing with your feet shoulder-width apart, left hand on left hip and right hand extended above your head, bend slowly at the waist to the left. Hold at the first point you feel tension in your waist. Repeat on the other side.

STRETCHING LEGS

- Lean over, placing your hands on the ground, with one leg bent at the knee at a right angle to the ground and your chest resting lightly on that thigh. Stretch your other leg behind. Press your hips down until you feel tension in the back leg. Alternate legs (see Figure 2a).

- From the above lunge position, straighten the front leg and put your weight on the back leg. Flex the front foot back and reach over the front leg with your body (see Figure 2b). You should feel stretching in the front leg. Alternate sides.

- Standing on your left leg, reach back and grab your right foot. Lift the heel of that foot to the buttock. Hold for a few seconds. You should feel the stretch in the front of the right thigh. Alternate legs (see Figure 3).

- Stand an arm's length from a wall. Put your hands on the wall. Slide one foot back about two feet. Keeping both heels flat on the floor, bend the front leg and lean forward, straightening the back leg to stretch the calf muscle. Hold a few seconds. Alternate legs.

[FIGURE 2a]

[FIGURE 2b]

Stretching the legs

[FIGURE 3]

Stretching the thigh muscles

- Sit with both legs extended in front of you. Reach toward the toes and hold. You will feel stretching in the back of your legs and your lower back.

- Still sitting, bring your feet toward your body. Place the soles of your feet together. Hold your ankles and use your elbows to press on the inside of both knees. Press the knees down and hold (see Figure 4). You will feel stretching in the groin.

- Sit with one leg tucked into the body and the other leg extended. Reach forward and try to touch the toes of the extended leg. You will feel stretching in the extended leg. Hold, then alternate legs.

[FIGURE 4]

Stretching the legs and groin

STRETCHING BACK

- Lie on your back. Bend one leg and hold it under the knee. Keep the other leg straight and on the ground. Hug the knee to your chest. Alternate. Then bring both knees into your chest and roll your head up to meet the knees. Hold for a few seconds. You will feel stretching in your lower back.

- While on your hands and knees, arch your back toward the ceiling like a cat would. Hold a few seconds, then relax your back until it is parallel with the floor. You will feel stretching in your middle and lower back.

STRETCHING THE WHOLE BODY

- Stand erect with the fingers of both hands intertwined in front of you. Lift your arms overhead as you turn your palms outward. Lift onto your toes and slowly let your arms reach to the sides and down as you come down off your toes. This is a good way to end your stretching. You will feel stretching from your toes all the way up through your back to the shoulders, arms, and fingers.

- Repeat stretching exercises in reverse order, if you like.

EXERCISE AND CONDITIONING

People who are in good physical condition are able to exercise vigorously because their hearts and other muscles are strong and durable, they have plenty of red blood cells, they use the air they breathe efficiently, and their bodies contain little fat tissue.

An excellent way to test your physical fitness is to participate in the President's Physical Fitness Challenge. Many schools across the nation participate in this challenge each year. You can ask your physical education teacher about this test if your school does not already participate in the program. Another way to determine whether or not people are in good physical condition is to have them do the tests of physical condition described in Experiment 1.1.

Materials:

-stopwatch, or clock or watch with a second hand

-yardstick or measuring tape

-running shoes and light clothing

-a partner

Here are some tests that can be used to determine physical condition. Please do not try any of these tests if you or others involved have not been participating in some type of physical activity over the last few weeks. Instead, begin some type of exercise program, such as walking, swimming, or jogging, and then use the tests to monitor your progress.

Before doing any of these tests, be sure you warm up and stretch your muscles to prevent any injury, as described earlier in this chapter. Be sure to cool down afterward.

ABILITY TESTS

Balance:

- Stand on your toes with your heels together, arms extended out in front of your body, with eyes closed for 20 seconds or longer.

- Stand on one foot with the other foot straight out in front of you. Hold your arms out front at shoulder height. Rise onto the ball of the foot you are standing on and hold for ten seconds.

Flexibility:

- Sit on the floor with your feet against a wall. Keep the feet together and the legs straight. Bend forward at the hips. Reach for the wall with closed fists. You should be able to touch the wall with your closed fists.

- Stand with your legs together and straight. You should be able to touch your fingers to the floor.

Arm strength:

- Lie facedown on the floor. Place your hands on the ground under your shoulders. The elbows should stay close to the body. Keeping the legs and body straight, press off the floor until the arms are fully extended and the body is completely off the floor. Girls should be able to do this once. Boys should be able to do it three times.

Upper body strength:

- Boys should be able to do 8–10 push-ups with hands at shoulder level and away from the body.
- Girls should be able to do 6–8 push-ups.

Muscular endurance and strength:

- Lie on your side on the floor. Lift your top leg up until your feet are about ½ to 1 meter (2 to 3 feet) apart. You should be able to do 10 lifts with each leg.

Leg power:

- Stand with legs together and toes just behind a line. Bend your knees and jump forward. You should be able to jump a horizontal distance equal to your height.

Muscular endurance:

- Lie on your back. Put your hands behind your head with the elbows out to the side. Have someone hold your feet on the floor with your knees bent and your feet a little over a foot from your buttocks. Raise your upper body so the elbow touches the opposite knee, right elbow to left knee, then left elbow to right· knee. Count each touch. Make sure your elbows return to the ground after each knee touch. See how many you can do in one minute. Table 1 gives a rough estimate of muscular endurance.

TABLE 1

An Evaluation of Muscular Endurance

Muscular Endurance	Number of elbow to knee touches in 1 minute	
	Adolescent boys	Adolescent girls
Excellent	over 45	over 35
Good	35–45	30–35
Average	20–35	20–30
Fair	15–20	10–20
Poor	10–15	0–10

Endurance of vigorous exercise:

- Run in place for 1 minute, lifting your feet up at least 10 centimeters (4 inches). If, after one minute, you feel out of breath and have a pulse of more than 100 beats a minute, you do not have good endurance for vigorous exercise.

Moderate exercise endurance (see Table 2):

- Run and/or walk for 1.5 miles. Make sure you pace yourself and only do this test if you have been regularly participating in some type of physical activity.

TABLE 2
Endurance levels for 1.5-mile run or walk

Endurance Level	Time in minutes to run/walk 1.5 miles Adolescent boys	Time in minutes to run/walk 1.5 miles Adolescent girls
Excellent	10.5 or less	11.5 or less
Good	10.5–11.5	11.5–12.5
Average	11.5–13.5	12.5–15.5
Fair	13.5–16.0	15.5–17.5
Poor	more than 16.0	more than 17.5

AEROBIC AND ANAEROBIC EXERCISE

Physical exercise is either aerobic or anaerobic, though some activities combine both. Anaerobic—without oxygen—exercise is short in duration and high in intensity. Aerobic—with oxygen—exercise is long in duration and lower in intensity.

Running to catch a bus, lifting a heavy weight, or sprinting 100 meters are anaerobic activities. Such activity requires short bursts of high energy, often without breathing. During anaerobic exercise, oxygen is not used to provide the energy needed. Only limited amounts of energy can be produced in the absence of oxygen. Consequently, anaerobic exercise can occur for only short periods. The higher the intensity of the activity, the shorter its duration. The body can use anaerobic energy sources for one second to three minutes. After that time, muscles use aerobic energy, which requires oxygen.

As will be discussed in Experiment 1.4, lactic acid is produced in muscles during anaerobic exercise. Its accumulation causes muscle fatigue. This is why lifting heavy weights or running full speed can only be done for a short time. After anaerobic activities, such as the 100-, 200-, or 400-meter sprints, 100-meter swimming events, gymnastics routines, football, volleyball, and weight lifting, athletes breathe heavily for some time. They have incurred what is known as an oxygen debt. The anaerobic exercise has left them with excess lactic acid. Their bodies respond by drawing more air into their lungs. The acid is then removed by reacting with the oxygen that enters their lungs and then their blood. When you exercise anaerobically, you tire faster and are more likely to have sore muscles after you stop.

For any activity that lasts more than two or three minutes, aerobic energy sources are needed. After the chemicals used for anaerobic energy are consumed, the aerobic sources, which require oxygen, must supply the muscles with energy. The oxygen reacts with a carbohydrate to release energy. For very long exercise sessions, the carbohydrate supply may be used up and fats or proteins will then be used to provide energy. Aerobic energy is more plentiful than anaerobic energy, and because lactic acid is not a substantial by-product of aerobic activity, it can go on for long periods of time. Eventually, the body does become tired from other factors, such as fuel depletion or dehydration.

Aerobic exercise conditions the heart and lungs. Working muscles need oxygen, so the body responds by drawing more air into the lungs. The heart beats harder and more efficiently, sending more oxygen-rich blood to the muscles. A stronger heart that contracts more forcefully and with fewer beats can deliver blood to the rest of the body more efficiently. A body with a stronger heart can do more work and exercise. The increased capacity for exercise benefits athletes and people engaged in fitness activities.

Aerobic activities include walking, jogging, swimming, aerobic dance, and skipping rope. Sports considered aerobic include soccer, volleyball, basketball, cross-country skiing, and running, to name a few. Aerobics can be defined as the use of large muscle groups for at least fifteen to twenty minutes while maintaining 60 to 85 percent of the body's maximum heart rate.

Many sports commonly considered to be aerobic, such as tennis and basketball, also have an anaerobic component. These activities require periodic vigorous bursts of action. Anaerobic training along with the regular aerobic training for these sports help the athletes endure fatigue. Even athletes in cross-country running can benefit from anaerobic training. A fast start or a sprint at the end of a race requires anaerobic energy. Anaerobic training can help prepare an athlete for these and similar circumstances.

Materials:

- stopwatch, or clock or watch with a second hand
- volunteers of different ages, weights, and gender

Choose a type of aerobic exercise you enjoy doing—brisk walking, swimming, cross-country skiing, jogging, inline skating, or bicycling. Do not use a competitive sport in your project because competition can increase stress and change your heart rate.

Take the tests included in Experiment 1.1 or take the President's Physical Fitness Challenge. Before you begin any exercise session make sure you warm up and stretch your body to help prevent injury. Be sure to cool down after exercising (see p. 12).

After warming up and stretching, do your enjoyable aerobic exercise for 30 minutes three to four times a week. To make sure you are working aerobically during your exercise, take your pulse at least once during the activity. For aerobic exercise, your heart rate should be 60 to 85 percent of your maximum heart rate, which is 220 minus your age. Therefore, a fifteen-year-old would have an aerobic heart rate of approximately 123 to 174.

$$220 - 15 = 205; \text{ and } 0.60 \times 205 = 123; 0.85 \times 205 = 174$$

You can check to see if you are at your target aerobic heart rate during exercise by stopping briefly to take your pulse for 10 seconds and multiplying by 6. Another simple but less accurate way to tell if you are working aerobically is your ability to talk while exercising. You should be able to carry on a short conversation while doing aerobic exercise. If you are gasping for breath while talking, you are probably working anaerobically.

Take your pulse before participating in the exercise and as soon as you finish. Also, take your pulse 30 minutes after exercising. Record your results over a period of at least six weeks. What are your three pulse rates (before, immediately following, and 30 minutes following exercise) after completing six weeks of aerobic exercise sessions? How do these rates compare to the same rates when you first started this project? What physical condition were you in before conducting this project? Check your results on the physical fitness tests (Experiment 1.1) after completing this exercise project. Did you improve your performance level on any of the tests? What could explain any changes you find?

Have a number of volunteers of different ages, weights, and gender do this experiment. Have them do the physical fitness tests before and after doing this experiment. How does six weeks of aerobic exercise affect their ability to do the physical fitness tests? Does their physical fitness before the experiment affect the changes in any of their three heart rates (before, immediately following, and 30 minutes after exercise)?

 Science Fair Project Ideas

- Compare different types of aerobic activities. For example, do you work as hard while walking aerobically as you do while jogging? Test your pulse during these different activities. Compare other types of aerobic activities, like swimming or bicycling.
- Try exercising at the high end of an aerobic activity (80 to 85 percent of your maximum heart rate) as compared to the lower end (60 to 65 percent of your maximum heart rate). How do your pulse rates at the two different levels compare? How much longer can you exercise at the lower level than at the higher level?

1.3 Anaerobic Exercise and Performance

Materials:
- stopwatch, or clock or watch with a second hand
- jump rope

Anaerobic exercise includes short periods of high intensity exercise, such as running, hopping, or skipping, separated by short periods of recovery time. It involves exercising at or near your maximum heart rate. The recovery rest period is slow jogging or walking. Remember to take into consideration your physical condition when you begin this experiment.

Take the tests included in Experiment 1.1 or take the President's Physical Fitness Challenge. Make sure you first warm up and stretch your body to help prevent injury. Be sure to cool down after exercising (see p. 12).

Take your pulse before you begin to warm up, at least once during the exercise session to make sure you are working anaerobically, and immediately after exercising. Then take your pulse 30 minutes after exercising. During anaerobic exercise, you should be working at over 85 percent of your maximum heart rate.

The anaerobic exercise can be done for 10, 20, or 30 seconds (choose one) by running, hopping, or jumping rope as fast as you can. If you run for 10 seconds, rest for 10 seconds. Repeat 20 times. If you decide to run, hop, or jump rope for 20 seconds, rest for 15 seconds and repeat the series 10 times. If you decide on exercising for 30 seconds, rest 1 minute and repeat the series 8 times.

For longer times of anaerobic exercise, run hard for 1 minute, rest for 4 minutes and repeat the series 5 times. Or exercise hard for 2 minutes, rest for 10 minutes and repeat the series 4 times.

Compare your pulse rates after doing the regimen 3 to 4 times a week for 6 to 8 weeks. Take the same tests you took at the beginning of your project and compare your results. Did the anaerobic training affect your results in any of the tests? Were you in good anaerobic condition when you began the training project? Could that have affected your results?

🏆 1.4 Tired Muscles

- 2 partners
- stopwatch, or clock or watch with a second hand
- graph paper

When the same muscle is used over and over again, it tires. The energy needed to make a muscle contract comes from chemical changes that occur in the muscle cells. One of the products of these reactions is lactic acid. Muscle fatigue is caused by the accumulation of lactic acid in the muscle cells. In aerobic exercise, the lactic acid is removed by the blood so that it does not accumulate, but anaerobic exercise of a muscle leads to its fatigue.

About 20 percent of the lactic acid eventually reacts with oxygen to produce carbon dioxide and water with the release of energy. The rest of the lactic acid is changed to glycogen, a starch that serves to store energy. Glycogen is readily changed to glucose sugar, which is a main energy source for the human body.

To see the effects of repeated use of muscles, stand with your right arm raised to shoulder height with your palm turned downward. Have a partner with a stopwatch act as timer. When you hear the timer say "Go," begin closing and opening your right hand to make as many fists as possible during a twenty-second period. Another partner will count the number of fists you make during the twenty-second interval. At the end of twenty seconds the timer will say "Stop!" At that point, you will drop your arm and rest for twenty seconds. The person who did the counting will record the number of fists you made during this first trial in a data table similar to Table 3.

After resting for twenty seconds, repeat the experiment with the same hand. Continue to do this until you have completed five trials with twenty seconds of rest between each trial. Then repeat the experiment with your left hand.

After you have completed your trials with both hands, have the timer serve as the subject, while you count and the counter becomes the timer.

28 ACE YOUR SPORTS SCIENCE PROJECT

TABLE 3

Data Table for Measuring Muscle Fatigue
(Number of Fists Made)

Subject's name	Trial 1	Trial 2	Trial 3	Trial 4	Trial 5

DO NOT WRITE IN THIS BOOK

Repeat the entire experiment three times so that all three members of the team serve as a subject.

Plot a graph of the number of fists you made in twenty seconds versus the number of the trial. Plot the data for both hands on the same graph. Have each subject plot his or her own data on a separate graph. How can you explain the results as depicted on the graphs? Are the results for both hands the same? If not, can you explain why?

Since lactic acid reacts with oxygen, you might expect that increasing the concentration of oxygen in the body would reduce lactic acid levels and help to prevent muscle fatigue. After an hour or more of rest, you can test this hypothesis. Simply repeat the experiment, but during all five trials and during the rest periods between trials, have the subject breathe deeply. That is, he or she should take in more air than usual with each breath. This will bring more air (and oxygen) into contact with the blood and thus provide more oxygen to the muscles.

Have all three subjects repeat the experiment. Record and graph the data for each subject. Do the experimental results tend to confirm or deny the hypothesis? Explain why you think so.

 ## Science Fair Project Ideas

- Repeat Experiment 1.4 with your arms at your sides rather than raised. Are the results the same? If they are not, explain why they are different.
- Investigate where and how glycogen is stored in the body.
- What is meant by "oxygen debt"? How is oxygen debt related to Experiment 1.4?
- Investigate the role of ATP (adenosine triphosphate) in muscle contraction.

Chapter 2

What Makes a Good Athlete?

BEING IN GOOD PHYSICAL CONDITION IS IMPORTANT FOR AN ATHLETE. Improving flexibility, building up strength and endurance, and increasing overall fitness are the ingredients to success in sports. But what else makes a good athlete? What is one of the basic qualities that scouts for professional teams look for in young players? The answer is speed!

Speed is the distance that something moves divided by the time it takes to move that distance. Speed can be represented mathematically by a simple formula:

$$\text{speed} = \text{distance} \div \text{time, or speed} = \frac{\text{distance}}{\text{time}}, \text{ or } s = \frac{d}{t}$$

You may think that speed and velocity mean the same thing; that is, distance divided by time. But there is a difference. Velocity is speed in a particular direction. If someone tells you a sprinter runs 10 meters in 10 seconds, you know the runner's speed is 1.0 m/s. But if she tells you a sailboat is traveling 1.0 m/s northwest, you know the boat's velocity. She has told you not only the boat's speed but also the direction in which it is traveling. To boaters, hikers, and bikers, it is more important to know velocity than speed. If you are traveling at the right speed but in the wrong direction, you will never reach your destination.

Materials:
- baseball field
- friend
- stopwatch, or watch or clock with a second hand
- tape measure

Covering ground as a fielder, stealing bases, and running the bases quickly is often the difference between winning or losing in baseball. Can a base runner round the bases at the same speed as a sprinter in track? You can find out by doing an experiment.

Find a baseball field and do some warm-up and stretching exercises. Then stand on home plate. Have a friend shout "Go!" as he or she starts a stopwatch or notes the time on a watch with a second hand or mode. When you hear "Go," run around the bases as fast as you can. Be sure to touch each base. Have your friend record the number of seconds it took you to round the bases.

The distance between bases is 90 feet. (On a Little League or softball field it is only 60 feet.) What is the total distance from home plate to first base, then to second and third base, and finally back to home plate? Is that the actual distance a player runs after hitting an inside-the-park homer?

Now walk at an even pace between home plate and first base. Count the number of steps you take. Then move to the outfield. Use the same even pace to mark off a distance that is four times as long as the distance from home to first base. For example, if you walked one hundred steps between home and first, measure off a distance that is four hundred steps long in the outfield. This distance should be very close to 360 feet, the same as the distance of the base paths.

Have your friend measure the time it takes you to run this distance. How does the time to run the straight-line distance (360 ft) in the out-field compare with the time it took you to run around the base paths in the infield? Based on the results of your experiment, can a base runner in baseball run as fast as a sprinter in track? If not, why not?

Science Fair Project Ideas

- Because you round the bases, you run farther than 360 feet when you hit an inside-the-park homer. Run the bases as if you had hit an inside-the-park homer on a field that has dirt base paths so you can see your footprints while someone times you with a stopwatch. Use a tape measure to determine the actual distance you traveled. What was your speed? How does it compare with your speed along a straight-line path of the same length? In addition to distance traveled, what else affects your speed in running the bases?

- James "Cool Papa" Bell, who played in the Negro Leagues before baseball was integrated in 1947, could round the bases in 13 seconds. Compare Bell's speed on the base paths with modern players. You can do this with a stopwatch at a game or on television. You do not have to wait for an inside-the-park homer; you can time doubles or triples and calculate the answer, considering the difference in distance.

- Compare Bell's speed on the base paths with the speed of modern sprinters who run 100 or 200 meter races. Explain why Bell's speed was slower, even though he might have won a race against these present-day sprinters.

Materials:
- baseball field
- 2 friends
- stopwatch, or clock or watch with a second hand
- baseball
- baseball glove

A good outfielder must be able to make fast and accurate throws to keep runners from taking an extra base or scoring. His or her throws must get back to the infield or home plate as quickly as possible. One of the most common mistakes among young players is the way they throw the ball from the outfield. They try to throw the ball to a catcher or baseman so that it is in the air when it reaches their teammate. In this experiment, you will find out why a different kind of throw is better.

Before you begin this experiment, be sure to do some stretching exercises, especially with your throwing arm. Then have a catch with someone to be sure your arm is warmed up. Once you are ready, stand in center field and get ready to make a throw to home plate.

One friend with a stopwatch should stand near home plate. A second friend will stand on home plate and act as your catcher. Your friend with the stopwatch will measure the time it takes the ball to reach home plate after it leaves your hand. He or she will then record that time in a notebook.

Your first throw should be made at an upward angle so that the ball reaches the plate and the catcher in the air without bouncing on the ground. For the second part of the experiment, throw the ball so that its flight is almost horizontal. The ball should take one or two hops before reaching home plate.

Repeat the experiment several times. Then, if possible, have several different people carry out the same experiment.

Which kind of throw takes less time to reach home plate? Should a long throw from an outfielder always reach an infielder in the air, or is it better if it bounces once or twice? Can you explain why?

Should throws to first base made by infielders bounce or travel entirely through the air? Explain your answer.

2.3 Are Passes Really Faster?

Materials:
- basketball, soccer ball, or 2 hockey pucks
- hockey sticks
- ice skates
- stopwatch, or clock or watch with a second hand
- basketball court, soccer field, or hockey rink
- several friends

Basketball coaches tell players with a fast break opportunity, "Pass the ball, do not dribble it up the court." Soccer coaches tell players, "Pass the ball, don't dribble it up the field." Hockey coaches tell players, "If possible, pass the puck. Don't carry it up the ice on your stick." Are these coaches right? The experiments that follow will help you to find out. You can do all the experiments, or you can choose to do the one connected with the sport you like best.

BASKETBALL

Do some warm-ups and stretching. Then stand on the end line at one side of a basketball court. Have a friend with a stopwatch stand at midcourt. At the moment your friend shouts "Go!" he or she will start timing. As soon as you hear "Go," dribble the ball as fast as you can toward the other basket. When you reach the midcourt line, your friend will stop the watch or note the time that has elapsed since shouting "Go." He or she will then record the time it took you to dribble the ball half the length of the court.

Now repeat the experiment. But this time, when you hear "Go," throw the ball up the court as hard as you can to a second friend standing at midcourt. Your first friend will note and record the elapsed time at the moment your second friend catches the ball.

Compare the time required to dribble the ball to midcourt with the time required to pass it the same distance. In which case, dribbling or passing, does the ball travel faster? Can you tell from the recorded times how many times faster it traveled?

Design an experiment to measure the average speed of the ball you dribbled and the one you passed. How do the two speeds compare? Do these two speeds agree with the ratio of the speeds you calculated from the two recorded times?

SOCCER

After warming up and stretching, stand on the goal line at one end of a soccer field with a soccer ball. Have a friend who is standing at the midfield line with a stopwatch shout "Go!" as he or she starts timing. When you hear "Go," begin dribbling the ball, under control, as fast as you can toward midfield. At the moment you reach midfield, your friend will note and record the elapsed time it took you to dribble the ball half the length of the field.

Stand at the goal line again with a soccer ball. This time, when you hear "Go," kick the ball toward the midfield line, where your partner is standing with the timer. Your friend will note and record the elapsed time when the ball crosses the midfield line.

Compare the time required to dribble the ball to midfield with the time required to pass it the same distance with a good kick. In which case, dribbling or passing, does the ball travel faster? Can you tell from the recorded times how many times faster it traveled?

Design an experiment to measure the average speed of the ball you dribbled and the one you kicked. How do the two speeds compare? Do these two speeds agree with the ratio of the speeds you calculated from the two recorded times?

HOCKEY

Warm up and stretch. Then stand on skates beside the goal mouth at one end of the rink with your hockey stick and a puck. Have a friend with a stick and puck stand at the blue line at the other side of the red line. Have a second friend shout "Go!" and observe both pucks. When you hear "Go," begin moving your puck forward by carrying it on your stick while skating to the opponent's blue line as fast as you can go. At the same time, upon hearing "Go," your friend will pass a puck toward the goal from which you are starting. Which puck traveled faster, the one you were carrying on your stick or the one your friend passed?

Design an experiment to measure the speed of the puck you carried on your stick and the speed of the one your friend passed. Remember: Speed is distance divided by time.

2.4 How to Kick a Football the Maximum Distance

Materials:

- football
- football field with lines
- garden hose or a high-powered squirt gun
- cardboard
- protractor
- level surface, such as a stand, garden table, or seesaw support
- a friend
- tape measure, meterstick, or yardstick
- marker

A football team's punter must know how to make a punt travel different distances. How hard the ball is kicked is one factor. But does the upward angle at which the ball is kicked also make a difference?

To find out, stand on the goal line. You can measure the distance your punts travel by watching to see the yard line on which they hit the ground (not the line to which they may bounce). Try punting a ball with the same force but at different angles to the ground, as shown in Figure 5.

Does the angle at which the ball is punted affect the distance it travels? If it does, approximately what angle makes the kick travel farthest? (Do not count any punts that are off the side of your foot or that do not spiral.)

You can determine the angle that produces the longest kick more accurately by doing another experiment. In this experiment, you can control the angle. Use a garden hose or a high-powered squirt gun that uses compressed air. Either device can launch water to represent a football coming off your foot. You can measure the angle at which the water is launched by making a large half-protractor on a sheet of cardboard, as shown in Figure 6.

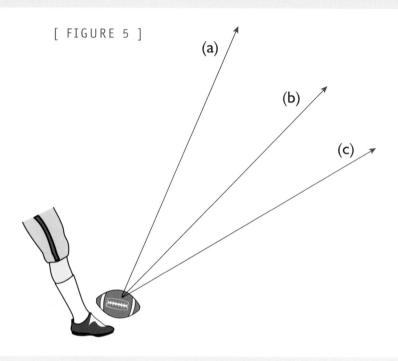

[FIGURE 5]

(a)

(b)

(c)

Kick the ball at different upward angles: a) a large upward angle; b) a medium upward angle; c) a small upward angle.

Place the giant protractor on a level surface. A stand, garden table, or seesaw support will provide a stable and level surface from which to shoot the water. As you know from kicking the football, speed, as well as angle, will affect the distance that the water will travel. So you want to be sure the speed at which the water emerges from the squirt gun or hose is the same for each angle at which you fire the water. You can do this by marking the point where the water lands when it is fired horizontally from the level surface. Test several times to be sure that point is approximately the same each time before projecting the water at different angles.

After establishing the fixed range for 0 degrees (level), launch the water at an angle of 10 degrees. Have a partner mark the point where the water lands.

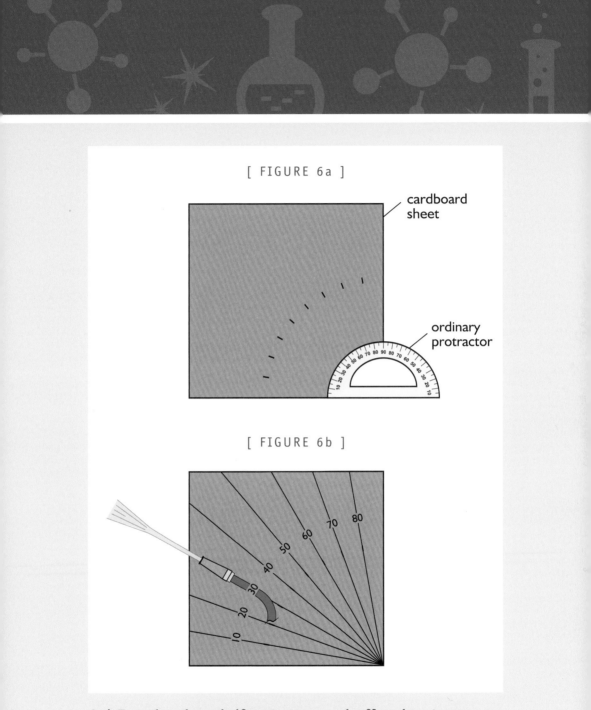

[FIGURE 6a]

cardboard
sheet

ordinary
protractor

[FIGURE 6b]

6 a) To make a large half-protractor, mark off angles at one corner of a large sheet of cardboard. This can be done with a small protractor, as shown. b) Then use a straight stick or yardstick to extend the lines. A hose or large squirt gun can now be used to launch water at known angles.

The distance from the launch site to the point where the water lands is the range for that angle. It can be measured with a tape measure, a meterstick, or a yardstick. Repeat the experiment for 20, 30, 40, 45, 50, 60, 70, 75, and 80 degrees. Why might it be wise to skip 90 degrees?

For which angle is the range greatest? Does this agree with the approximate angle that caused your kicks to travel the farthest? Are there angles for which the range is very nearly or exactly the same? If there are, what are these angles?

Materials:

- grassy area where ground is soft and flat
- a friend

The center of gravity (COG) of any object is the point where all its weight can be considered to be located. It is the point from which the object, if suspended, will be balanced with no tendency to rotate. Every object has a COG, but it is not necessarily at the center of the object. An understanding of center of gravity is important in most sports.

Football players are coached to take a wide stance (feet apart) and keep the center of their bodies low when they get into position. When tackling an opponent, they are often instructed to keep their eyes on a point several inches below the center of the ball carrier's waist. Players who carry the ball are told to run with a wide base and to stay low.

Soccer players are coached to take a wide stance while heading a ball, to keep the center of their bodies low when approaching an offensive player with the ball, and to watch a point several inches below the center of that offensive player's waist.

Hockey players are told to keep their skates as far apart as the width of their shoulders, to keep the center of their bodies low when approaching an offensive player with the puck, and to watch a point several inches below that offensive player's waist.

Is there a good reason for such coaching tips? Why are players coached to run and position themselves in this way?

To see what such coaching tips have to do with your COG, stand on a soft, grassy area with your feet together. Ask a friend to give you a shoulder-level push to one side. What happens?

Repeat the experiment, but this time stand with your feet spread well apart. Why are you more stable in this position?

Repeat the experiment once more, but this time stand with your feet spread well apart and your knees bent so that your body is much lower. Why are you even more stable in this position?

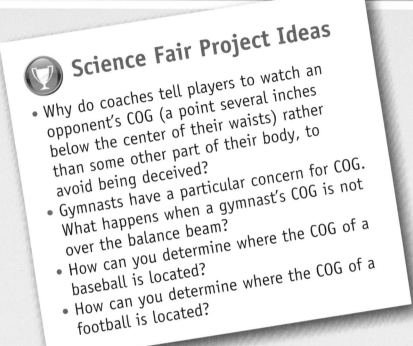

Science Fair Project Ideas

- Why do coaches tell players to watch an opponent's COG (a point several inches below the center of their waists) rather than some other part of their body, to avoid being deceived?
- Gymnasts have a particular concern for COG. What happens when a gymnast's COG is not over the balance beam?
- How can you determine where the COG of a baseball is located?
- How can you determine where the COG of a football is located?

2.6 A Football's Center of Gravity and Passing

Materials:
-football
-large field
-several friends

When someone says "ball," you probably think of a sphere—something round like a globe. Most of the balls used in sports are round. The game of football is different. It is played with a ball that looks like two fat miniature canoes that have been glued together. Throwing or kicking a football is a whole different ball game. To make a football travel far and true requires skill.

The COG of a spherical ball is at its center, but a football is not a sphere. Its COG is inside the ball at the center of the circle around the ball's fattest part. If you punt a football by bringing your foot against the ball's COG, the ball will "float"; it will not rotate. Try punting a ball this way. You will see that it floats and does not travel very far.

Throwing a football requires skill. Try throwing it with your hand behind the ball's center of gravity (COG). To throw a football so that your hand pushes through the ball's COG, place your hand perpendicular to the ball's longest axis, at its fattest part. When you throw the ball this way, you will be pushing along the ball's COG. Throw the ball to a friend. Notice that the ball floats like a knuckleball in baseball.

How far can you throw a football when you throw it with your hand directly behind its COG? How accurately can you throw the football?

Now throw the ball as a quarterback would. Grasp the ball by its laces at points behind its COG, as shown in Figure 7a. If you throw the ball that way, you can make it spiral; that is, you can make the ball spin about the long axis through its COG, as shown in Figure 7b.

How far can you throw a football when you throw a spiral? How accurately can you throw the football when you make it spiral? Can you throw farther and more accurately when you make it spiral than when you throw a "floater"?

If possible, repeat the experiment with different people throwing the football. Are the results the same?

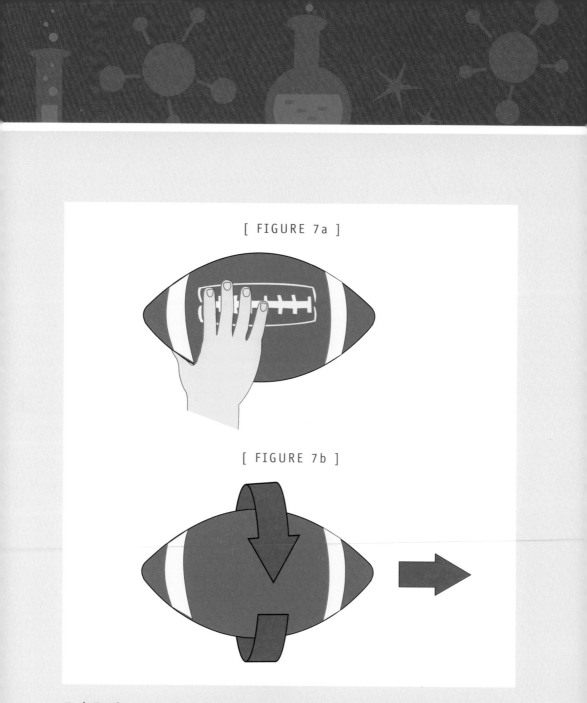

[FIGURE 7a]

[FIGURE 7b]

7 a) To throw a spiral, hold the ball by its laces at points behind its COG.
b) With this grip you can throw a spiral; that is, you can make the ball rotate about its COG.

Science Fair Project Ideas

- If a force is applied at any object's COG, a football or anything else, the object will not rotate. To throw a spiral as a quarterback does, a force must be applied at some distance from the COG. Such a force causes the ball to rotate about its COG. The same thing happens when you pull on the rim of a wheel that is free to spin.

- Any object rotating about its COG is said to have angular momentum. Carry out an investigation to find out what momentum and angular momentum have to do with the constant rotation of a thrown football. What role does gravity play when a football is thrown?

- How does the pointed shape of a football affect its flight through the air from passer to receiver? Are there differences?

Baseball and softball players talk about the "sweet spot" on a bat. The sweet spot is the place on the bat where the batter likes to make contact with the ball. It feels good when you make contact with the ball on the sweet spot. If the bat collides with the ball at other points, the bat vibrates. In cold weather, the vibrations may cause the batter's hands to sting. If the bat vibrates, some of the kinetic energy (the energy associated with motion) you use to hit the ball goes into the vibrating bat rather than into the ball. When you hit the ball at the sweet spot, the maximum amount of kinetic energy is transferred to the ball, so it will go farther.

Is the sweet spot at the same place as the bat's COG? You might guess that it is. In this experiment you can find the sweet spot and see for yourself if the COG and sweet spot are one and the same.

To begin, find the COG of a baseball or softball bat by balancing the bat on your index finger, as shown in Figure 8a. Use a marking pen to mark the bat's COG.

Next, find the bat's sweet spot, the spot where there are no vibrations when the bat and a ball collide. Hold the bat with your fingers loosely surrounding its narrow end. The bat should be free to swing, as shown in Figure 8b. With a hammer, tap the bat gently at a point close to its fat end. You will feel the bat's vibration in your fingertips. Continue tapping the bat at different places with the hammer. When you tap the sweet spot, you will feel no vibration.

Mark the location of the sweet spot on the bat with a marking pen. Is the bat's sweet spot located at the same place as its COG?

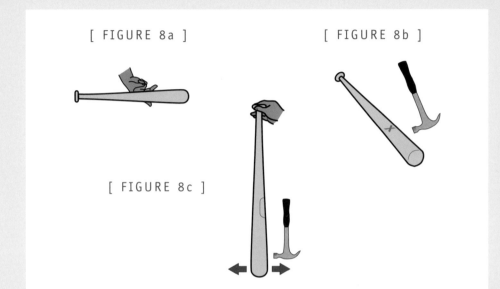

[FIGURE 8a]

[FIGURE 8b]

[FIGURE 8c]

8 a) **Find a bat's COG by balancing it on your finger. b) You can find the sweet spot on a bat by tapping it gently with a hammer. c) How does the bat move when you hit it at its COG? How does the bat move when you hit it at its sweet spot?**

Science Fair Project Ideas

- Place the bat on the floor. Use a hammer to tap the horizontal bat at its COG (see Figure 8c) How does the bat move when you strike it on its COG? How does it move when you strike it at the sweet spot?
- Can you explain why the bat moves as it does when you hit its COG? Can you explain why the bat moves as it does when you hit its sweet spot?

Materials:

- soccer ball
- soccer field and goal
- tape measure
- pail
- flour, baby powder, or sticks
- 2 friends

If you have ever played pool, you may have learned that shooting the ball in the pocket requires an understanding of angles. Billiards is not the only game in which playing the angles is important. Every sport involves angles. Sometimes it is the angle from which one has to shoot a ball or a puck toward a goal. It may be the angle from which a throw must be made, or the best angle for a tackler to pursue a runner.

Distances are important, too. Soccer players like to be as close to the goal as possible when they shoot. But defenders try to make them shoot from greater distances and from difficult angles. From what distance or angle is it best to shoot for a goal? This experiment will help you answer this question.

Generally, the percentage of successful shots in soccer is related to the angle from which the shot is made. As you will find in doing this experiment, the width of the open goal that is visible decreases as the angle increases. What effect does angle have on shooting success? This experiment will help you to find out.

A soccer goal is 8 yards wide, but you seldom see the entire goal open. To make the shooting more realistic, place a pail 2 yards from one goal post, as shown in Figure 9. Then measure out the shooting positions for different angles, as shown in Table 4. Stand at those numbered positions, as shown in Figure 9, and take shots at the 2-yard opening between the goal post and the pail. The angle between the center of the open goal line and the point where the shot is made is indicated in Table 4. The positions are all 15 yards (45 ft) from the center of the 2-yard-wide goal. To find

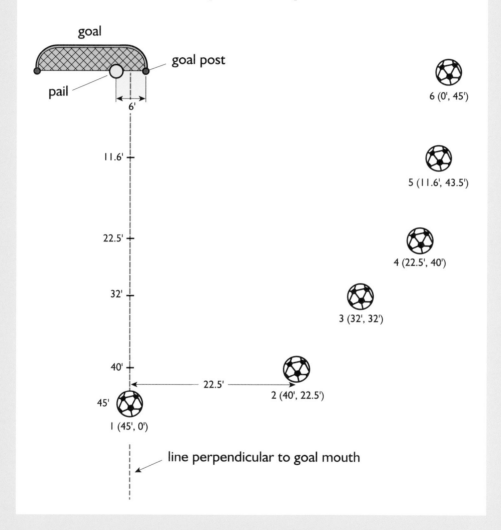

[FIGURE 9]

Position numbers and distances are indicated on the drawing. The numbers in parentheses are, first, the distance along a line perpendicular to the goal mouth, followed by the distance to the right of that line. All shooting positions are 45 feet from the goal mouth. Similar positions can be established on the other side of the line perpendicular to the goal.

the positions for each angle, begin by marking a line perpendicular to the center of the 2-yard-wide goal. All positions will be measured along this line and then along lines perpendicular to this line as shown on Figure 9 and as indicated in Table 4.

Use flour (or baby powder or sticks) to mark the positions for the various angle shots on the field. Then take about five or six shots from each position. Have a friend record the shots taken and made from each angle. Another friend can return the ball to you.

Then let your friends try the same experiment while you record results or return shots.

TABLE 4
How to set up positions for angle shots

Position Number	To establish a shooting angle of	Measure a distance along a line perpendicular to the mouth of the goal that is	Then measure a distance perpendicular to the first line that has a length of
1	0	45.0 ft	0
2	30	40.0 ft	22.5 ft
3	45	32.0 ft	32.0 ft
4	60	22.5 ft	40.0 ft
5	75	11.6 ft (11 ft, 7 in)	43.5 ft
6	90	0	45.0 ft

What is your percentage of success from each of the angles where you took shots?

What happens to the percentage of shots made as the angle to the mouth of the goal increases?

Is there any way to kick a goal when the angle is 90 degrees and no part of the open goal can be seen?

Science Fair Project Idea

Design and carry out an experiment to find out how distance from the goal affects the percentage of shots made. Should there be an active goalie while you conduct this experiment?

Chapter 3

Sports and Physics

IN CHAPTER 2, YOU LEARNED ABOUT THE BEST PATH TO TAKE WHEN RUNNING THE BASES. You learned how and where to throw, shoot, or pass. You also learned that the center of gravity is important in sports. In this chapter, momentum, follow-through, collisions, Magnus forces, and the Bernoulli principle will be introduced. You may be surprised to find out that you can learn a lot about physics through sports. Understanding physics may allow an athlete to better understand some of the instructions given by his or her coach.

The momentum of a ball or of any moving object is its mass times its velocity (mass × velocity, or mv).

$$\text{Momentum} = \text{mass} \times \text{velocity, or } M = mv$$

If you have a mass of 50 kilograms (kg) and are running at a velocity of 6 meters per second (m/s), your momentum is 300 kg m/s.

The momentum of a ball (or any object) depends on the impulse it receives. Impulse is the product of the force applied to the ball and the time that the force acts.

$$\text{Impulse} = \text{force} \times \text{time, or } I = Ft$$

If a net force of 100 newtons (N) acts on you for 3 seconds, you receive an impulse of 300 N/s.

Since an object receives its momentum from the impulse applied to it, the two quantities are equal; that is:

$$\text{Momentum} = \text{Impulse, or } mv = Ft$$

The greater the impulse applied to an object, such as a ball, the greater its momentum. You know that when a force acts on an object at rest, the object accelerates in the direction of the force. As the velocity of the object increases, so does its momentum. As long as the force acts, the object continues to accelerate. Consequently, the longer a certain force acts on a ball, the more momentum the ball acquires.

Suppose a force, F, is applied to a ball for a time, t. The ball acquires a certain momentum, mv that is equal to Ft. You can give the ball the same momentum by applying a force twice as big for half as much time. Or you can give the ball the same momentum by applying a force half as big for twice as long.

If you tried to stop a car rolling slowly along a level surface, you could not stop the car quickly because you are not strong enough to apply a force big enough to stop the car in a short time. However, if you tied a rope to the car and pulled back against its motion, you could eventually bring it to rest.

3.1 What Is the Importance of Follow-Through?

Materials:
- an adult if using <u>outdoor ice</u>
- soccer ball
- large field or lawn
- hockey rink or smooth, frozen lake or pond
- hockey stick
- hockey puck
- football
- kicking tee (optional)

Coaches often tell players to "follow through!" But what does *follow through* mean, and how important is it? From what you know about impulse and momentum, you may be able to figure out the scientific meaning of follow-through by doing some experiments related to different sports. You can begin with soccer.

FOLLOW-THROUGH AND SOCCER

One way to discover the effect of following through is to kick a soccer ball. Kick the ball with your instep as you normally would during a warm-up period. That is, kick the ball with a fluid, but not swift, leg motion and continue to move your foot and leg forward and upward after it makes contact with the ball.

Next, kick the ball without following through. Stop your foot's motion at the moment it makes contact with the ball.

Make a few more kicks, some with good follow-through, and others without follow-through. Does following through increase the distance the ball travels?

If you are a soccer goalie, how can you do the same experiment by throwing the ball with and without follow-through?

FOLLOW-THROUGH AND HOCKEY

Hockey coaches tell players to "follow through" when they shoot the puck. They mean keep the stick on the puck for as long as possible. Do not stop driving the puck midway through the process of shooting. As you shoot, shift your weight from your rear foot to your front foot. This will increase the speed of your shot.

To see the effect of following through while shooting a hockey puck, begin by shooting the puck as you normally would in making a slap shot. That is, draw your stick back to the height of your hips, swing it into the puck, and turn your wrists so as to keep the stick against the puck for as long as possible. As you move the stick and your arms forward after striking the puck, shift your weight from your rear foot to your front foot just as you would if you were throwing a ball.

Next, shoot the puck without any follow-through. Stop the motion of the stick and your arms and the forward transfer of your weight at the moment the stick makes contact with the puck.

Make a few more shots, some with good follow-through, and others without follow-through. How does following through affect the speed of the puck?

FOLLOW-THROUGH AND FOOTBALL

Another way to see the effect of following through is to punt a football or kick it from a kicking tee. After you have stretched and warmed up, punt a football or kick it from a tee as you normally would in a game. That is, kick the ball with a fluid forward leg motion that continues after your foot makes contact with the ball.

Next, kick the ball without following through. That is, stop your foot's motion at the moment it makes contact with the ball. Do not continue to move your foot through the ball after the initial contact.

Make a few more kicks, some with good follow-through, and others without follow-through. Does following through increase the distance the ball travels? How is follow-through related to the impulse you apply to the ball?

Science Fair Project Ideas

- Examine follow-through as it applies to tennis, table tennis, basketball, baseball or softball, lacrosse, golf, and other sports of your choice.

- Learn about Newton's first law of motion. Using your knowledge of impulse, explain why the results of pulling a sheet out from under an object are so dependent on the size of the force you apply. In addition to impulse, what other factors are involved?

- Now that you are familiar with forces, momentum, and impulses, think about the effect of soft and hard surfaces on running speed. Explain why athletes run more slowly on soft fields than on hard fields. How is the time for a runner's foot to come to rest with each step related to the firmness of the field's surface? How is the upward force on the athlete's foot affected by the softness or hardness of the field's turf?

Materials:
- an adult if using outdoor ice
- baseball glove
- a friend
- baseball
- soccer ball
- hockey sticks
- hockey pucks
- hockey rink or smooth, frozen lake or pond

Catching or trapping a ball is part of many sports. Coaches often say that players who catch or trap well have "soft hands" or "soft feet." What do coaches mean by "soft"?

Find out what it is like to be on the receiving end of a pass in a number of different sports. You might begin with baseball, where catching is the fundamental defensive part of the game.

CATCHING AND BASEBALL

Put on a baseball glove. Ask a friend to throw you a baseball with moderate speed. **(DO NOT try this experiment with a fastball!)** Keep your hand and glove in a fixed position as you catch the ball.

Repeat the experiment, but this time let your hand, arm, and glove move with the ball as you catch it (see Figure 10). This is the way someone catches a baseball if he or she has no glove—the way a smart fan in the bleachers catches a foul ball. It is the way a first baseman catches a hard throw or the way any fielder catches a line drive.

Repeat the experiment a few times. Which method of catching the ball—stiff- or loose-handed—requires you to apply a bigger force to the ball? How can you tell? In which case did it take longer to make the catch? How do you know?

"Soft Hands"

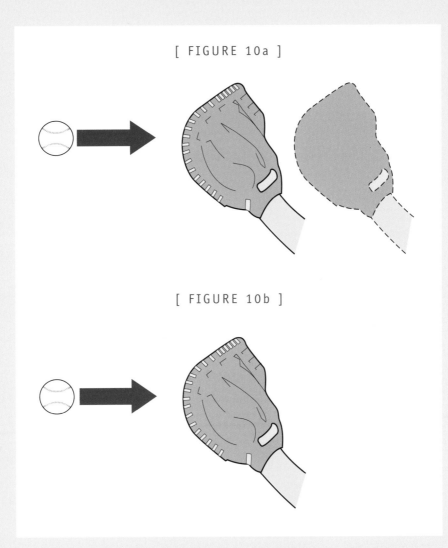

[FIGURE 10a]

[FIGURE 10b]

10 a) To increase the time that you apply a force to a ball as you catch it, let your hand and glove move with the ball. b) A rigidly held glove will reduce the time you apply a force to the ball in catching it.

In both ways of catching the ball, you transferred the ball's momentum—its mass times its velocity—to your body and ultimately to the earth on which you stood. In both cases you applied a force to the ball. In both ways of catching the ball, the force acted on the ball for a short interval. In both ways of catching the ball, you applied an impulse—a force times a time—to the ball. When you caught the ball by moving your arm, hand, and glove with the ball, you increased the time that the force acted on the ball. Which method of catching the ball took the sting out of the catch? Why? Which method of catching the ball reduced your chances of dropping it? Why?

CATCHING, TRAPPING, AND SOCCER

Like baseball and football players who are adept at catching balls, a good soccer goalie must have soft hands, too. Of course, soccer players who are not goalies are not allowed to use their hands except on throw-ins, but they do have to trap balls with their bodies, legs, and head. It would not be right to say they have soft bodies, and certainly not soft heads, but they do have to let their bodies, legs, or heads move with the ball as they trap it.

To see why they do, ask a friend to throw or kick a soccer ball to you. The ball should travel at a moderate speed. Keep your body or leg in a fixed position as you trap the ball. **DO NOT try to trap the ball with your head in this way!**

Repeat the experiment, but this time let your body or leg move with the ball as you trap it.

Repeat the experiment a few times. Which method of trapping the ball required you to apply a bigger force to the ball? How could you tell? Why should you let your body, legs, or head move with the ball when you trap it?

In both ways of trapping the ball, you transferred the ball's momentum—its mass times its velocity—to your body and ultimately to the earth on which you stood. In both cases you applied a force to the ball. In both ways of trapping the ball, the force acted on the ball for a short interval. In both ways of trapping, you applied an impulse—a force over time—to the ball. When you trapped the ball by moving your leg or body with the ball, you increased the time that the force acted on the ball. Which method of trapping the ball felt better? Why? Which method of catching the ball reduced your chances of losing it to an opponent? Why?

RECEIVING A PASS IN HOCKEY

A hockey goalie catching a puck is similar to a catcher receiving a fastball, but the other members of a hockey team receive the puck in a very different way. Stand on a hockey rink or any smooth, icy surface, with a hockey stick in your hands. Ask a friend to use his or her stick to pass a puck swiftly along the ice to you. As the puck reaches your stick, use your arms to keep the stick in a firmly fixed position on the ice. What happens to the puck when it hits your stick?

Repeat the experiment, but this time let the stick move with the puck as you receive it. What happens to the puck this time?

Repeat each method of receiving the puck a few times. In which method of receiving the puck—with a fixed stick or a loose-handed stick—do you apply a bigger force to the puck? How can you tell? Which method of receiving the puck takes longer? Which is the better way to receive a puck? Why?

In both ways of receiving the puck you transferred the puck's momentum—its mass times its velocity—to your body through the stick and ultimately to the earth through your body. In both cases you applied a force to the moving puck. In both ways of receiving it, the force acted on the puck for a period of time. In both ways of receiving the puck, you applied an impulse—a force over time—to it. When you received the puck by letting the stick "give" with the puck, you increased the time that the force acted on the puck. In which method of receiving the puck did you feel less force on your hands through the stick? Why? Which method of receiving the puck reduced your chances of losing it to an opponent? Why?

COLLISIONS IN SPORTS

Collisions are common in sports. Collisions between players are part of the game in football and hockey. Collisions between balls and bats occur in baseball and softball. Collisions between balls and racquets constitute the games of tennis, squash, and racquetball. Collisions between a ball and a surface are part of any game played with a ball.

For a collision to occur, one or more of the objects that collide must be in motion. During collisions, impulses are applied to bring about changes in momentum. There are also energy transformations during a collision. Part of the energy of motion (kinetic energy) may be changed to elastic energy within the materials that bump into one another. For example, when a ball collides with a floor, materials within the ball are squeezed together (compressed) during the collision. This is similar to a spring being compressed. Energy is stored in the spring. It reappears as the spring returns to its normal length. As the elastic material in a ball returns to its normal shape during the rebound, some of the elastic energy is changed back to kinetic energy. The rest appears as thermal energy (the ball becomes warmer).

If all the kinetic energy is restored after a collision, the collision is said to be elastic. Collisions among gas molecules or between gas molecules and the walls of their containers are completely elastic. We do not have to add energy to keep them from slowing down. If all the kinetic energy is lost during a collision, such as the collision between a lump of clay and the floor, the collision is said to be totally inelastic. Many collisions are partially elastic, meaning some kinetic energy is regained after the collision.

Materials:

- hard floor surface
- meterstick or yardstick
- baseball
- Superball
- tennis ball
- basketball
- marble
- clay
- paper
- pencil
- calculator (optional)

It is useful and easy to determine a number for a ball that describes how well it bounces. With such numbers, you can make a list of balls in their order of bounciness. You have already taken some measurements of bounces. They can be used to assign a rebound rating to each ball. (The rebound rating is called the rebound ratio in some sports science books.)

The rebound rating is the length of the rebound divided by the length of the drop. For example, in an experiment with the everyday rubber ball, the following measurements were obtained.

Length of drop: 160 cm (63 in)

Length of rebound: an average of 96 cm (37.8 in)

The rebound rating for this rubber ball is $\dfrac{96 \text{ cm}}{160 \text{ cm}} = 0.60$.

This value shows that the ball bounced back up to a height that was six-tenths (0.60 or 60 percent) of its starting height of 160 cm.

The rebound rating depends on the particular ball, on the height from which it is dropped, and on the surface on which it lands. As long as the balls are dropped from the same height onto the same surface, their bounces can be compared. Thus, you have a way to compare the bounciness of balls.

Now that you have learned about the rebound rating, you can use it to compare how balls bounce.

Set a standard height for all your measurements of rebound ratings. Your standard height should be between 5 and 7 feet. Also, all the bounces should be made on the same hard surface, such as wood, tile, asphalt, or smooth cement.

Make up a table of rebound ratings for any balls that you test. Add to this table whenever you test other balls.

What are the rebound ratings for the following balls: baseball, Superball, tennis ball, basketball, marble, and small clay ball?

Which ball bounces the highest (has the highest rebound rating)?

Which is the least bouncy (has the lowest rebound rating)?

Rank all the balls you have tested so far in order of their bounciness.

Appendix 1 gives the sizes and rebound ratings of the balls examined in this book. The official requirements for the rebound ratings are given where the professional association has specified them. Otherwise, the balls were dropped from a height of 60 inches onto ceramic tile.

Science Fair Project Ideas

- If you throw a ball forcefully to the floor, it will collide with the floor at a higher speed than if you just dropped it. As a result, it may have a different bounce height. Another way to increase the collision speed is to drop the ball from higher up. Compare the rebound ratings of the same ball when dropped at different speeds. Find out if other balls behave similarly. How does this affect performance in a game?

- How is the flattening of a ball on collision with the ground connected to bounciness? How might you estimate how much flattening occurs?

3.4 Rules for Game Balls

Materials:

- soccer ball
- cloth tape measure
- balance
- pressure gauge
- basketball
- 2 metersticks or yardsticks
- tape
- different surfaces, such as wood, tile, or concrete
- field
- valve used to inflate soccer ball
- air pump

According to the rules, a soccer ball must have a circumference (distance around) of 67–71 centimeters (27–28 inches), a weight of 397–454 grams (14–16 ounces), and be inflated to a pressure of 0.63–0.74 kilograms/square centimeter (0.6–0.7 atmosphere, or 9.0 to 10.5 pounds per square inch).

Find a soccer ball and use a tape measure to determine its circumference. Does the ball's circumference meet the requirements of the rule?

Use a balance to weigh the ball. How much does it weigh? Does the ball's weight meet the rule?

Using a pressure gauge, measure the air pressure inside the ball. What is the air pressure? Does it meet the rule?

In basketball, the rules require that the ball must have a certain "bounciness," or elasticity. As described in the rules of the game: *When dropped to the playing surface from a height of 1.8 meters (6 feet), measured to the bottom of the ball, it should rebound to a height measured to the top of the ball of not less than 125 centimeters (49 inches) or more than 137 centimeters (54 inches).*

Find a basketball. Then tape two metersticks or yardsticks together end to end and test the ball to see if it meets the bounciness rule described above. Repeat the experiment several times to make sure the results are nearly the same each time. How high does the ball bounce? Does the ball you tested have the bounciness required by the rules?

Does the surface on which the ball lands affect its bounce? To find out, try dropping the same ball on different surfaces. You might try wood, concrete, tile, macadam, and so on. What do you find?

As you have seen, a basketball must bounce to a height that lies between 5/9 and 5/8 of the height from which it is dropped. (Remember, a basketball is about 9 inches in diameter.) Is a regulation soccer ball as bouncy as a regulation basketball?

To find out, hold a soccer ball that meets the rules' requirements so that the bottom of the ball is level with the top of a yardstick or meterstick. Release the ball onto a wooden or tiled floor. Watch the bottom of the ball closely. How high does it rise after it hits the floor? Repeat the experiment several times to make sure the results are nearly the same each time. To what fraction of its original height does the ball rise? How does the bounciness of a regulation soccer ball compare with the bounciness of a regulation basketball?

To see how field conditions affect the bounciness of a soccer ball, repeat the bounciness test on parts of a field that are covered with: (a) tall, thick grass; (b) short, thick grass; (c) soft dirt; (d) hard-packed dirt; (e) mud. (If the field is dry, ask the owner's permission to soak a small area near the edge of the field with water to make it muddy.)

The valve used to inflate the ball can also be used to release most of the air from a regulation soccer ball. After some of the air has been released, repeat the test for bounciness. How does reducing the air pressure within the ball affect its bounciness? How does it affect the weight of the ball? Can you explain why it changes the weight?

Pump the ball back to its original pressure. Then add more air to the ball. How does increasing the pressure affect the bounciness of the ball?

Materials:

- an adult

- uncooked eggs

- firm, hard surface, such as a floor or sidewalk

- various materials, such as cotton, newspapers, small boxes, tape, rubber bands, elastic bands, etc.

- yardstick or meterstick

Collisions between players are part of the game in hockey and football, but they occur in other sports as well. Baseball players are told by their coaches to call for a fly ball by yelling, "I got it! I got it!" The reason for the call is to prevent collisions between fielders. An infielder calling for the ball is supposed to give way if he hears an outfielder calling for the ball. Why do you think the outfielder is the preferred player? Despite their calls, baseball players do sometimes collide, and sometimes are injured as a result.

Player collisions are also common in basketball, soccer, lacrosse, even doubles tennis. Despite the danger, football was originally played without helmets, and professional hockey players, even goalies, were not required to wear helmets for many years. Today's players are better protected because they do wear helmets and other protective equipment. But how do helmets reduce head injuries?

Your brain is surrounded by a bony skull that protects it. A thin layer of fluid between the brain and the skull serves as padding so that the brain will not slam against the hard skull. In this experiment, you will use an egg to represent the human head. The egg's shell corresponds to the skull; the fluid inside the egg represents the brain.

Your task is to design and build a "helmet" for the egg so that it will not break when it falls to the floor or ground from a height of 2 meters (about 7 feet). After designing the "helmet," gather the materials you need and build a helmet to fit the egg.

Once you have built the helmet, test it by dropping it and the egg within it from a height of 2 meters (about 7 feet) onto a hard surface. If the egg does not break, you have designed a good helmet.

You might organize a contest to see who can build the best helmet for an egg. For those whose eggs survive a 2-meter fall, **ask an adult to help you** extend the test to 3 meters (10 feet) or higher. What do you find are the key factors in building a good helmet? What scientific principles related to impulse (force x time) are involved in designing and building a satisfactory protective helmet?

 Science Fair Project Ideas

- Examine the protective equipment worn by football players, such as helmets, shoulder pads, rib pads, thigh pads, and so on. How do they reduce injuries caused by collisions between players, and between players and the surface on which the game is played? How are these pieces of protective equipment related to the scientific principles of momentum and impulse?
- What common injuries related to football and other sports are not reduced by protective equipment? How might these types of injuries be diminished?

3.6 What Is the Magnus Effect?

Materials:

- string with length of 91 cm (3 ft)
- wide, strong rubber band
- baseball
- table or drawer

Another principle of physics important to sports is the Magnus effect. It applies to many of the balls used in sports and is of profound importance. Without the Magnus effect, a golf ball could not travel far and a tennis ball could not dip sharply to land unexpectedly inside the court. Ping-Pong balls, volleyballs, soccer balls, and basketballs also show a Magnus effect.

Scientists have long sought to unlock the secret as to why the Magnus effect takes place. How does it work and how does each kind of ball activate it? Today, we have some answers.

For years, experts claimed that no pitcher throws a curveball and that curveballs were optical illusions. Scientists have since taken measurements that show that the ball does indeed curve. A baseball can be made to curve as much as 48 centimeters (19 inches) away from a straight line between the pitcher's mound and home plate (18.4 meters or 60.5 feet) to the front edge of the plate.

Why do curveballs curve? A baseball thrown without spin flies off with practically no curve except for the descent caused by gravity. In order to make a ball curve, the pitcher must throw it so that it spins in flight. When a spinning ball moves through air, a force develops that is greater on one side than on the other. The greater force pushes the ball to the side. The force is called the Magnus force after Gustav Magnus (1802–1870), who published a scientific article on it in 1853 (see Figure 11).

You can observe the Magnus effect by spinning a baseball on a pendulum.

Obtain about 91 centimeters (3 feet) of soft string (such as the white string used to wrap bakery boxes). Slip one end of the string under a wider, stronger rubber band that fits tightly around a baseball.

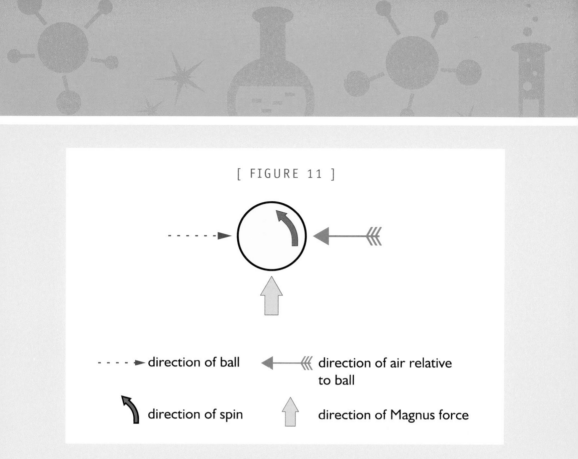

[FIGURE 11]

- - - - ▶ direction of ball   ◀——⟨⟨ direction of air relative
                                                to ball

direction of spin   ⬆ direction of Magnus force

How a curveball curves: the Magnus effect

Hang the other end of the string from a support (open drawer handle or tabletop) so that the ball hangs freely. It is important that the support does not move at all during the experiment.

Draw the ball back and let it go to check that it swings back and forth in a straight line. Stop the motion.

Twist the string for 50 or more turns. This is most easily done by slapping the ball to keep it going around. When the string is twisted, catch the ball with your hand to keep it from untwisting.

Pull the ball straight back as before and release it. Observe the path. To which side is the ball pushed outward?

When the baseball swung back and forth without spin, its path did not curve. The spinning baseball was different. Its path began to curve after a few swings. As it moved forward, the path of the spinning baseball curved as shown in Figure 12.

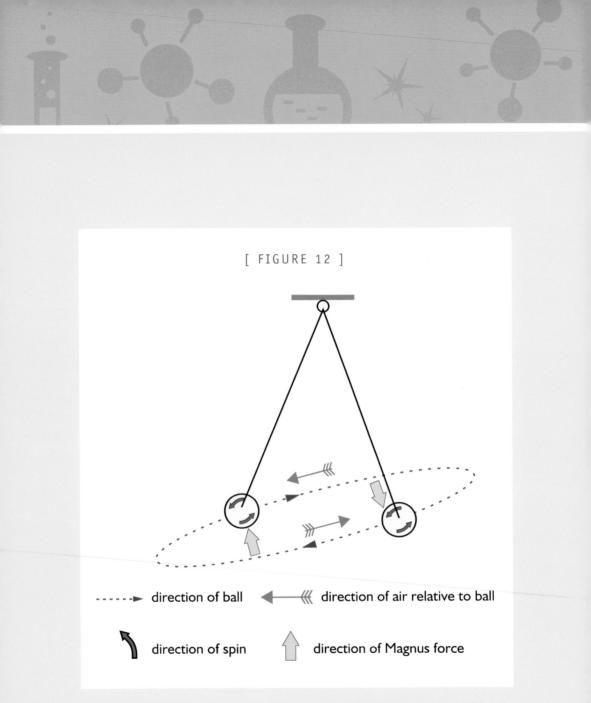

[FIGURE 12]

- - - - - -► direction of ball   ◄———◀◀◀ direction of air relative to ball

direction of spin   ⬆ direction of Magnus force

A pendulum with a spinning ball can illustrate the Magnus effect. The curve is exaggerated.

The narrow oval of the swing was not large, but it was distinct. As can be seen from Figure 12, the Magnus force pushes outward on the side of the ball where the spin goes in the opposite direction to the airflow. This results in the ball being pushed outward when the pendulum swings in one direction, and outward again when the pendulum reverses. Hence, a loop forms. What causes the Magnus force?

Magnus measured the air pressures on both sides of a spinning object while air was flowing past it and found that there was a difference in pressure on the two sides. The greater pressure acted as the force that pushed the ball.

How does the Magnus force develop on a baseball? When a baseball moves through the air, a layer of air (the boundary layer) is held between the stitches and spins with the ball as it rotates. As the spinning ball moves through the air, the air layer on one side of the ball is moving in the same direction as the air through which it passes; the air on that side of the ball speeds up. On the other side of the ball, the boundary layer is moving opposite to the motion of the air that the ball is traveling through; the two motions oppose each other, so the flow of air on that side slows.

It is the difference in the speed of the air on opposite sides of the spinning ball that causes the pressure difference. The effect of air pressure difference on two sides of an object was first discovered by Daniel Bernoulli, a Swiss scientist (1700–1782). He found that the faster air exerts less pressure on the object. Slower air exerts more pressure on the object. So the slower air pushes the object to one side.

The spinning boundary layer held by the stitches on the baseball interacts with the passing air to cause the path of the ball to curve.

Materials:

- 2 baseballs
- 2 rubber bands
- 2 strings, each at least 61 cm (2 ft) long
- table or drawer
- paper cut into 5-cm (2-in) squares
- straight pin
- tape
- spool

Circle a strong rubber band around a baseball. Attach a string to the baseball by tucking one end under the rubber band. Do the same for a second baseball. You can do this with any two balls (tennis balls, oranges, Ping-Pong balls, etc.).

Hang the baseballs by their strings so that they are about 10 centimeters (4 inches) apart. You can suspend them from the top of an open drawer or from a table. They should be able to swing freely.

From up close, blow strongly between the two balls. What do you observe?

Did the baseballs fly apart? No! The baseballs bumped together. The air on the outer side of each ball was standing still. The air between the balls was moving. Which exerted more pressure, the moving air or the still air? Because the balls were pushed together, the outer air had to be pushing harder. Bernoulli was right. The pressure of the moving air was lower than that of the still air. The higher pressure of the outside air pushed the baseballs together.

Here is another example of Bernoulli's principle. Stick a pin into the middle of a 5-cm- (2-in-) square piece of paper. Push it in all the way. Tape the head of the pin in place. Hold the square over the top of a spool (the spool need not have thread on it) with the pin sticking into the hole. The pin is there to keep the square from sliding out of place over the hole (see Figure 13).

Hold the spool so that you can blow strongly upward through the hole. Try it.

Did the square blow off and fall to the ground?

The rapidly moving air blown into the spool was at a lower pressure than the still air outside of it. The still air on the other side of the paper was at a higher pressure. The higher pressure pushed the square of paper against the spool so that it could not fall off the spool.

As a simple rule, the ball will curve in the direction that it spins as it moves forward. The wake shifts to follow the ball in its new direction.

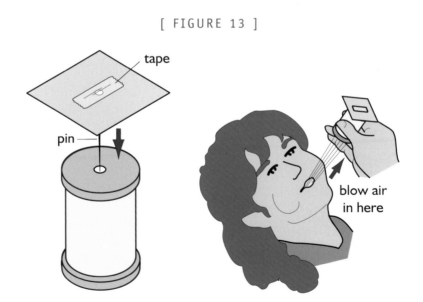

[FIGURE 13]

tape

pin

blow air in here

Bernoulli's principle: Air is blown through the bottom of the spool up to the piece of paper. Does the paper fall off the spool?

The Magnus force (boundary layer effect) helps make many sports such as golf, tennis, and baseball much more exciting. In the remainder of this book, reference will be made again and again to the Magnus force.

Most major-league pitchers throw curveballs. Even the fastball is also a curveball. The pitcher causes the ball to curve by the grip and by a snap of the wrist as the ball is released. The position of the fingers on the ball determines the direction of the spin, because they cause friction against the seams. The faster a pitched ball spins, the greater its curve. If the ball curves only horizontally, the batter will still be able to hit it but at a different spot on the bat. Curves that break both horizontally and vertically are needed. Figure 14 shows just a few of the many grips that a pitcher uses to throw balls with a curve.

[FIGURE 14]

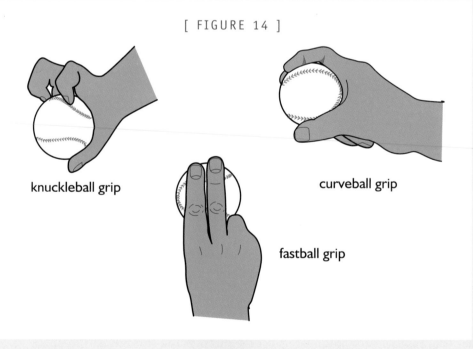

knuckleball grip

curveball grip

fastball grip

Pitchers may use many different handgrips to pitch curveballs.

Science Fair Project Ideas

- You can use a giant pendulum to explore Magnus forces. By making the pendulum as long as you can, changes are easier to observe. The number of rotations per second that the spinning ball makes can be altered by using different strings to support the ball, such as a rubber band, thicker string, or stiff string. Does it make a difference if the string is twisted for one hundred turns compared to fifty turns? For each experiment, keep all the variables the same except for the one you are testing.

- Scientists have found that the Magnus force also operates on smooth balls but only at high speeds and to a much smaller degree than when there is a boundary layer. In some cases, the ball curves in the direction opposite to that which occurs with a baseball. Investigate and compare the direction of the curve for a smooth ball and for a baseball. Do the same for the magnitude of the curve.

- Pitchers can throw a fastball so that the ball rotates with the seams (two-seam grip) or across the seams (four-seam grip). The four-seam grip develops more turbulence and therefore more ball movement. However, many pitchers believe that the two-seam grip is less predictable and prefer to use it. By attaching the pendulum string to different spots on a baseball, you can change the orientation of the seams as the ball spins in its path. Orient the ball on the pendulum so as to simulate the four-seam and two-seam grips. How is the flight of the ball affected? Try other orientations.

Chapter 4

Tennis and Golf

TENNIS AND GOLF MAY SEEM STRIKINGLY DIFFERENT FROM THE OTHER SPORTS DISCUSSED SO FAR IN THIS BOOK. But this chapter will show you that many of the principles that apply to other sports also apply to tennis and golf.

As you get older, you may find that it becomes more difficult to play sports like soccer, football, and baseball. Learning how to play tennis or golf while you are young will allow you to enjoy them when you are older. Many people continue to participate in these sports throughout their lifetime. Like the sports discussed in earlier chapters, these sports also have a long history in our country and other parts of the world. While methods, practices, and equipment have seen a lot of change, some things have remained the same. Be sure to keep in mind the concepts discussed earlier in the book as you do the experiments in this chapter.

Materials:
- tennis racket
- tennis ball
- tennis court with net

Modern tennis began indoors as a sport for French royalty during the reign of Louis X (1314–1316). Although today's game is quite different, our scoring system dates back to then; the scores represent minutes coming full circle in time: 0, 15, 30, 40 (an abbreviation for 45), and 60. About 1870, when rubber balls that could bounce on grass were made, tennis became an outdoor game and rapidly gained popularity. Because a rubber ball is slippery, a flannel cover was made for it; that became today's fuzzy tennis ball cover. The fast, hard-hitting game of tennis today is played around the world by people at all social levels on all kinds of surfaces. Wimbledon, the oldest of all of today's tennis tournaments, began in 1877 for men and in 1884 for women.

The standards in the United States for a tennis ball are set by the United States Tennis Association (see Appendix A). The ball is made up of two concave rubber halves cemented together. The fuzzy cover is a combination of wool and synthetic fiber, often nylon. Any seams on the ball must be stitchless.

Which is bigger, a tennis ball or a baseball? Which bounces higher, a tennis ball or an ordinary rubber ball? If you have not yet obtained your own rebound rating for a tennis ball, this is a good point at which to measure it and to enter the result into your table.

One of the most powerful strategies of the expert tennis player is to put spin on the ball, to change both the flight of the ball and its bounce. As long ago as 1671, spin on a tennis ball in flight was already of interest to scientists. It was at that date that Sir Isaac Newton (1642–1727), possibly the greatest scientist of all time, wrote that he had seen a tennis racket cause a tennis ball to fly in a curved line.

A spinning tennis ball curves in flight due to the Magnus force (see Chapter 3). As with a baseball, both a boundary layer and spin are needed to make the ball curve. For a tennis ball, it is the fuzz that holds the boundary layer in place.

Flight of a Tennis Ball

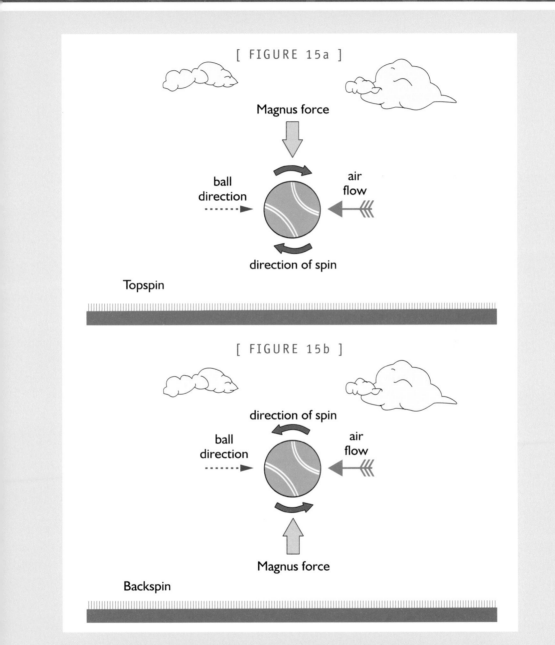

[FIGURE 15a]

Magnus force

ball direction

air flow

direction of spin

Topspin

[FIGURE 15b]

direction of spin

ball direction

air flow

Magnus force

Backspin

Spin on a tennis ball in flight. a) Topspin (forward spin) causes the ball to dip. b) Backspin (underspin) causes the ball to rise.

Unlike a baseball, which is usually pitched with sidespin, tennis balls are most often hit with topspin or backspin. With both topspin (also called forward spin) or backspin (also called underspin), the ball is spinning around a horizontal axis. The top of a top-spinning ball is moving in the same direction that the entire ball is moving, as shown in Figure 15a. With backspin, the top of the ball is moving in the opposite direction to the forward movement of the entire ball, as shown in Figure 15b.

To impart topspin and backspin, the racket has to slide across the ball in special ways.

A forehand stroke can be made to produce topspin. For a right-handed player, the racket starts upward from low at the right side. It moves up to strike the ball and to continue over it toward the left shoulder. If you are an inexperienced player, this may be difficult to do. If so, ask an experienced player to demonstrate it. How does the ball behave compared with when it is hit at a right angle to the racket?

Next, impart backspin to the ball to make the ball spin backward. To do this, a right-handed player uses a backstroke. The racket is held high to the left and is then brought down "through" the ball on a gradual decline toward the right hip. Again, you may want to ask an experienced player to demonstrate the stroke so that you can observe the flight of

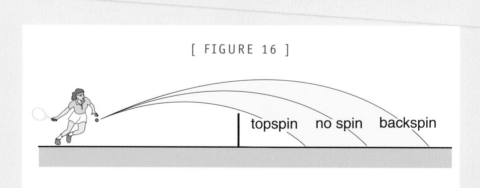

[FIGURE 16]

topspin   no spin   backspin

You can see the effect of spin on a tennis ball. The vertical heights are exaggerated to make the effect easier to see.

the ball. How do the flight of the ball and the distance covered differ from when it was hit with no spin?

Next, compare the results of hitting the ball with topspin, no spin, and backspin, but this time be careful to use about the same force on each. Figure 16 shows what would happen.

Topspin causes the ball to sink. Backspin causes the ball to rise in flight. How do you explain these in terms of the Magnus force? The Magnus force will not cause a ball to curve unless it has both spin and a boundary layer. It is the fuzz on the tennis ball that holds its boundary layer in place. The fuzz also makes the ball less slippery and adds to the air drag. The fuzz helps determine the nature of the tennis game.

Materials:

- partner
- coin
- hard, flat surface
- tennis ball

Have a partner stand 1.8 to 2.4 meters (6 to 8 feet) away on a hard, flat surface; place a coin on the floor between you. Have your partner throw a tennis ball without spin directly toward the coin from various distances while you catch the ball. Look at the angle to the ground that the ball makes on its approach and compare it with the angle of rebound. Anticipate where to stand to catch the ball. What rule did you follow?

When there is no spin, the ball bounces away from the ground at about the same angle that it was thrown toward it.

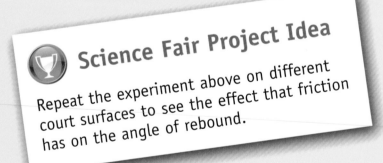

Science Fair Project Idea

Repeat the experiment above on different court surfaces to see the effect that friction has on the angle of rebound.

Materials:
- tennis ball
- hard, smooth surface
- tennis racket
- tennis court with net

When there is no spin on the ball, it is easy for the opposing player to judge how the ball will bounce and to deliver a powerful return shot. With spin, the story is very different. With spin, the rebound angle is theoretically affected, as shown in Figure 17. The speed of rotation and the ground surface friction affect how great the change will be in the rebound angle.

You can observe some of the effects of spin on the bounce by spinning the tennis ball with your hands as you let it fall to a hard, smooth surface. First, do it with topspin. How does the ball bounce? Repeat, but use backspin. How did the ball bounce this time?

Drop a tennis ball and, as it bounces back up, give it spin with a tennis racket by stroking it downward at one side. What kind of spin is this? What happens to the bounce? Once you get the knack, you can continue bouncing and hitting the ball sideways each time to keep it going. Try to spot which way the seams of the ball move.

Hold a racket horizontally at the center ribbon of the tennis net. Make sure the face of the racket is parallel to the net. The upper rim of the racket should be at the top edge of the net. Press a tennis ball between the middle of the racket and the center ribbon. With a sharp upward motion of the racket, roll the ball up and over the top to bounce on the other side. What happens to the bounce? Were you giving the ball topspin or backspin?

When you rolled the ball up the side of the net, the top of the ball was spinning in a forward direction as it went over the top. That was topspin.

Based on your observations, how do topspins and backspins affect the bounce of the tennis ball?

Topspin can give the ball a lower rebound angle, whereas backspin raises the rebound angle. Such changes in angle confuse the opponent planning to hit back a perfect shot.

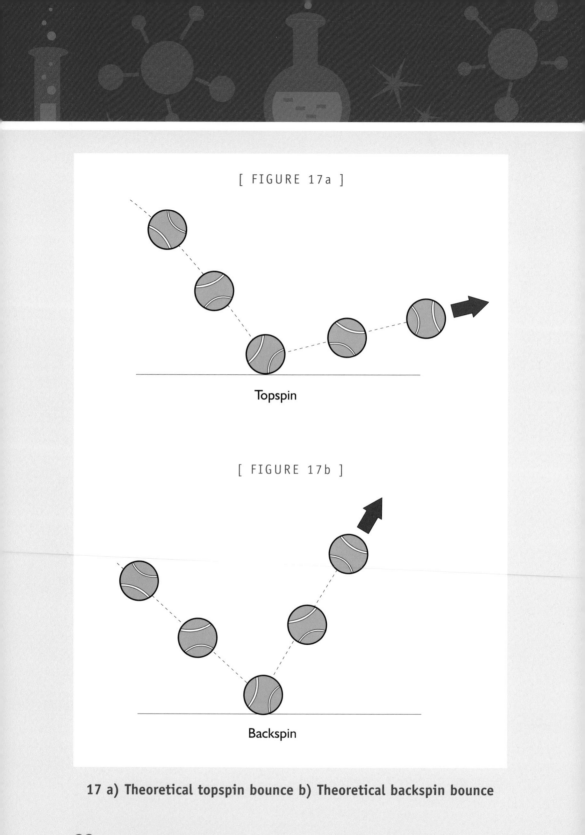

[FIGURE 17a]

Topspin

[FIGURE 17b]

Backspin

17 a) Theoretical topspin bounce b) Theoretical backspin bounce

In actual play, the story is much more complicated because other variables can also affect the bounce. Friction always gives the ball some forward spin because contact with the ground slows down the bottom of the ball. Ball speed, spin rate and direction, and whether the shot is slightly off center all interact with friction to affect the bounce. With four different variables interacting, the effect of spin on the bounce tends to become unpredictable during play. The player must depend on rapid reflexes.

Science Fair Project Idea

Tennis ball machines that impart spin are available at some tennis courts. Observe how spin affects the flight. How is this change affected when the speed of the ball is increased? How is this change affected when the speed of spin is increased? If no tennis ball machine is available, you can instead have someone hit tennis balls to you while you return the ball so as to give it spin. What happens as you change the speed of the ball? What happens as you change the direction of the spin?

4.4 What Is the Air Resistance

Materials:

- golf ball
- golf practice ball (available at sporting goods store)
- golf club (not a putter)
- large open field (or driving range if permission to do experiment is granted by owner)
- partner

Golf was first played in its modern form in Scotland over four hundred years ago. The earliest golf ball was wooden and was soon replaced by the featherie. Featheries were made of boiled goose feathers stuffed into a cowhide cover. When the feathers dried, the ball was hard and elastic. A featherie could be driven 150–175 yards, although it was useless when wet. Unfortunately, even the best workers produced only four to five a day. This limited golf to the wealthy such as Mary, Queen of Scots (sixteenth century), who was an avid golfer.

Featheries were made for about two hundred fifty years. About 1848, balls appeared that were made from inexpensive gutta-percha (a dried, rubbery gum from the sapodilla tree). However, they tended to break apart if not hit right in the middle. In 1898, the resilient rubber-core ball was invented. The game quickly spread all over the world.

Today, there are three types of balls in general use. The one-piece ball is made of a synthetic molded plastic and is used in driving ranges. It has a lower rebound rating than layered balls. The two-piece ball has a solid polymer core (acrylate or resin) with a durable cover. It gives good distance but is somewhat difficult to control. Three-piece balls are

of a GolF Ball?

made of a tough cover, a wound rubber yarn or polyurethane body, and a small core. The cores are adjusted to increase the weight of the ball to the allowed limit.

The modern golf ball is the most highly researched of all sports balls. That is because American industry manufactures so many of them—more than one billion golf balls each year.

Carry out this experiment in a large open field with no one else around except a partner. Otherwise, do it at a driving range but obtain permission from the owner first. A golf practice ball looks like a golf ball and is available at any sporting goods store. It is the same size as the golf ball and has dimples. However, it is filled with air.

Throw the practice ball as far as you can. Then, throw the golf ball as far as you can. Repeat until you are confident that you have observed the typical behavior of the balls.

Compare the horizontal distances covered before the first bounce (this distance is called the carry). Why are there differences in carry?

A golf ball carries much farther than a golf practice ball. This is why the practice ball is useful. It allows the golfer to practice hitting in a small area. Why does it go a shorter distance? The weight of the practice ball is much less. Given the same size balls, the effect of air drag (air resistance) is greater on the lighter ball. Drag is the friction between the air and any object moving through it. This friction causes the ball to slow down, so it does not go far before gravity pulls it to the ground. It is much easier for the heavier ball to dig a tunnel through the air than it is for the lightweight ball. The lightweight ball has more drag.

THE GOLF CLUB

Examine a full set of golf clubs. If you do not know someone who has a set, you can find one at any sporting goods store. What is a golf club? There are two types of clubs. How do they differ? How many are there of each type? Each club has a number at its end. How do the clubs change as the numbers increase?

Golfers are allowed to carry fourteen different clubs in a bag. Each club has a long, thin shaft that the golfer grasps at the thicker end. At the other end of the shaft is a heavy metal or wooden head. The front of the golf club head is called the face. One club is always the putter; the metal head has a vertical face. The putter is used to roll the ball along the ground and, hopefully, into the cup. The other clubs have faces that are angled. They are used to strike the ball up into the air. The No. 1 club has the lowest angle, about 10 degrees. As the club number increases, the angle of the face increases to up to about 50 degrees.

The two types of clubs are the irons, which have narrow metal heads, and the woods, which have large, solid, bulbous heads. Today, these are usually made of plastic or metal rather than wood.

Science Fair Project Idea

Test a golf ball to see how its rebound rating is affected by an increase in speed. You can increase the speed of the ball by simply dropping it from higher up, such as from a second-story window. Do this **under adult supervision** and be sure that no one is nearby who can be hit by the ball as it drops and bounces. Also be sure that the ball cannot do damage when it hits. What did you find? How does this affect the game of golf? Test other balls used in sports to see how an increase in speed affects the rebound ratings. How do they compare to the golf ball?

Materials:
- full set of golf clubs
- golf ball or ball of aluminum foil
- golf shop with rubber wall (or net)
- driving range or other safe place to hit golf ball

Why does the golfer use so many clubs? What difference do you think the angle of the club face makes? Why are there both irons and woods?

You can find the answers by working with the clubs. Many golf shops have an indoor area where you can safely hit the ball with a club into a rubber wall or net. Hit some balls with each club to see how the golf club operates. You can instead hit a ball of crumpled aluminum foil on a lawn where no one is near you. Obtain permission to use the lawn, because the club may dig a hole into the ground. Another safe place to practice using the golf club is at a golf driving range. Keep in mind that the putter is stroked along the ground, and all the other clubs are used to hit the ball hard up into the air.

Now that you have tried hitting some balls, what is your conclusion about the effect of the increasing angle of the club head? Why do you think that the golfer has so many clubs?

The answer is that the golfer controls the distance that the ball goes by the club selected. It would be possible, instead, to hit the ball with the same club each time and to hit it harder or softer as needed, but this is very difficult to control. By using different clubs, each club can be swung with about the same force. The distance that the ball goes depends on the angle of the club face. As the number of the club goes up, the angle at which the ball takes off (the launch angle) increases (see Figure 18). With increasing launch angle, the ball swoops higher into the air (loft), flies a shorter distance horizontally (carry), and rolls for a shorter distance because it descends more sharply.

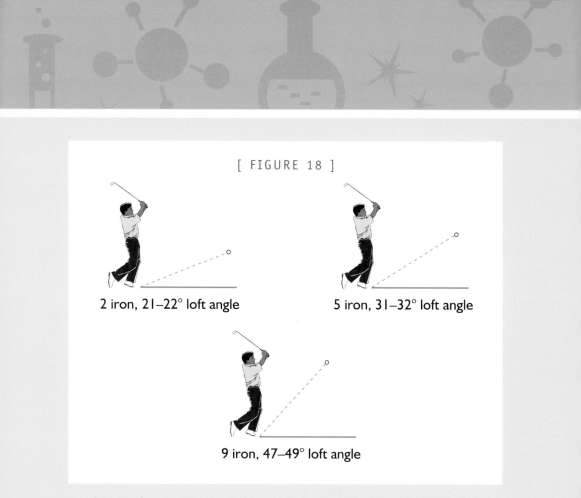

[FIGURE 18]

2 iron, 21–22° loft angle

5 iron, 31–32° loft angle

9 iron, 47–49° loft angle

As the number on the golf club increases, the angle at which the ball takes off also increases.

The farther the ball needs to go, the lower the club number chosen. The woods are usually used when a very long distance is needed. This is because the woods have the longest club shafts and the heaviest heads.

High ball speed requires high club head speed. The almost explosive collision when the club head slams into the ball takes place in less than one-thousandth of a second. The blink of an eye takes almost one thousand times as long. During that contact time, the ball moves a little less than one inch. A club head that was going at 100 miles per hour slows to 81 miles per hour. The energy from the club head goes largely to compress the golf ball. A little energy is changed to sound. The ball flattens to an oblong shape about one-third of its usual diameter. Then it springs back into shape. Some of its energy is changed to heat as it does so. The expanding golf ball pushes backward on the club head. This push further slows the club head to about 70 miles per hour, and the club head pushes the much lighter ball up to about 135 miles per hour. Ball speeds in professional golf today average 150 miles per hour.

The angled face of the club head not only lofts the ball but also causes backspin. This is of great importance to the distance covered, as will be discussed later. When the ball is hit, it starts sliding up the angled club face. Friction causes the ball to rotate backward as it slides, so the ball takes off with backspin. The higher the angle of the club, the more spin on the ball.

Science Fair Project Idea

The ground speed of a ball is different from its speed along the line of flight. The ground speed is obtained by dividing the horizontal distance (the carry) a ball travels from impact to landing (it does not include the roll) by the time it takes. Measure the ground speed of balls hit with the same impact by club faces with different angles. How does the ground speed of a ball depend upon the club used?

Chapter 5

Baseball, Basketball, and Football

SOME MAY ARGUE THAT BASEBALL, BASKETBALL, AND FOOTBALL ARE THE MOST POPULAR SPECTATOR SPORTS IN OUR COUNTRY. These sports each boast a major league and have lots of fans. Certainly, the athletes involved earn high salaries and are well known in our country.

As you will see in this chapter, each of these sports has its own history and has changed over time. Though a ball is required for each of these sports, the balls come in different sizes and shapes and are made of different materials. Despite the differences, however, each requires athletes to be fit, fast, and coordinated. The athletes must train hard and practice often. Understanding the science behind the sport can help in hitting, catching, throwing, kicking, dribbling, shooting, and running!

BASEBALL

Play baseball on a baseball diamond with several friends. Instead of using a baseball, use a tennis ball. How does it affect the pitch? The catch? The bounce? Why?

You probably found that the pitcher needed to practice throwing, even though he may have been a very experienced baseball player. This is because a tennis ball is lighter than a baseball. You may also have noticed that when the lighter ball was hit by the bat, it did not go as far as expected. Finally, the tennis ball may have bounced clear away on landing because of its higher rebound rating. Each game depends very much on its ball.

HOW BASEBALL WAS STARTED

A persistent myth of baseball is that the game was invented by Abner Doubleday and was first played in Cooperstown in 1839. Sports historians today say that just is not true. Baseball arose out of two other games, the British game of cricket and a child's game called rounders. The earliest form of today's baseball appeared in New York City in 1845 when Alexander Joy Cartwright banded a group of young men together to form the New York Knickerbocker Baseball Club. Cartwright and Daniel "Doc" Adams drew up a set of rules that established baseball. Almost at once, the game began to spread rapidly.

The ball used was so light that it could not be thrown far. In the 1860s, Doc Adams remedied this by having a horsehide cover made for the ball. He stuffed it with three to four ounces of rubber cuttings, wound the cuttings with yarn, and then covered it with the leather. Today the ball is still made with layers, according to the old practice.

Baseball Measurements
5–5.25 oz
2.9-in diameter
0.32 rebound rating when fired at 85 ft/sec at a wall of ash boards backed by concrete

5.1 What Is a Baseball?

Materials:
- baseball, well worn
- measuring tape
- scissors

Obtain a used baseball and measure its circumference. How many stitches are on the baseball? Carefully cut the stitches and take the baseball apart. Roughly estimate the length of the pieces of yarn in it. Draw the two pieces that make up the cover of the ball in your science notebook.

Can you put the baseball back together again? What parts of it are crucial to how the ball behaves in a baseball game? What parts could be changed without much effect on play?

If you take a baseball apart, you will discover a round cork core surrounded by firm black rubber with red rubber over that (see Figure 19a). The entire core is almost 3.6 centimeters (1.4 inches) in diameter.

Wound over the core are yards and yards of clean white wool yarn with outside windings of many more yards of polyester-cotton blend. The total yardage is almost a quarter of a mile. The yarn is covered by a thin layer of latex adhesive.

The outside covering is made of two pieces of cowhide that are sewn together by 108 red cotton stitches laced over one edge and under the other (Figure 19b). The stitches bump up from the otherwise smooth surface of the ball. Because no machine has ever been invented that can stitch the baseball together, the stitches are always sewn by hand. The finished baseball is 23 to 24 centimeters (9 to 9.5 inches) around.

The following is what happens to a baseball when a fastball is pitched and hit.

- A pitcher's fastball could be moving at a speed of 145 kilometers per hour (90 miles per hour).
- The ball travels from the pitcher to the batter in about 0.5 seconds.
- The bat is in contact with the ball for about 0.01 seconds.

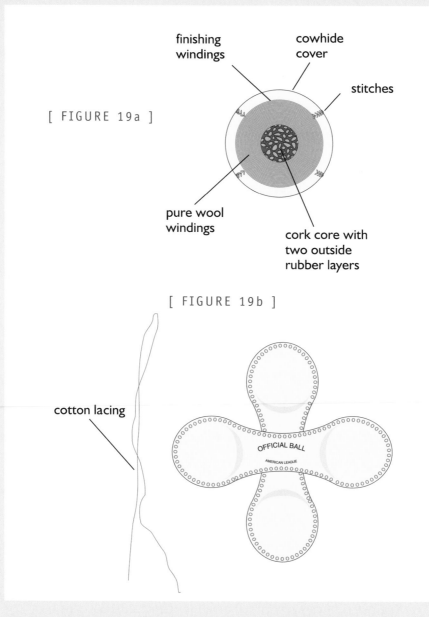

[FIGURE 19a]

finishing windings

cowhide cover

stitches

pure wool windings

cork core with two outside rubber layers

[FIGURE 19b]

cotton lacing

OFFICIAL BALL

AMERICAN LEAGUE

19 a) Cross-section of a baseball b) Two cowhide pieces make up the cover of a baseball.

- A well-hit ball is compressed by the bat to about half its original diameter, while the bat is compressed about 1/50 as much as the ball is compressed.

- Much of the energy of motion when the ball hits the bat is converted to heat; about 35 percent of the energy that the pitched ball had remains.

- As the batter slams the ball, energy of motion is transferred from the bat to the ball.

- When the bat exerts a force on the ball, the ball exerts an equal force on the bat, slowing the batter's follow-through. Because the bat is much heavier than the ball, its speed is changed only a little compared with that of the ball. Some of the bat's energy of motion is also decreased by friction with the air and by deformation (the bat is compressed on impact and then springs back to shape).
A ball that is traveling at 145 kilometers per hour (90 miles per hour) when it is hit may be batted back at 177 kilometers per hour (110 miles per hour).

The home team gives the umpire ten dozen new balls before each game. About 80 baseballs are used during an average major-league game (18 scuffed ones are tossed out, 60 are fouled out, 2 go into the stands on home runs). Roughly 200,000 balls are used during a major-league season.

5.2 Best Angle of Launch

Materials:

- garden hose with nozzle
- transparent protractor
- sheet of white cardboard about 22 x 25 cm (8 x 10 in)
- glue
- pencil
- ruler
- faucet (to connect garden hose to)
- partner

What is the best angle to launch a ball so that it goes farthest? Does the best angle change with the speed of the ball? The following will help provide answers.

In this experiment, a stream of water from a garden hose will be directed to go as far as possible. The distance depends on the angle from the horizontal at which the water shoots out from the nozzle—the launch angle.

To measure the launch angle, make a giant protractor (actually half a protractor) as follows. Obtain a small transparent protractor and glue it as shown in Figure 20a to a sheet of white cardboard about 20 x 25 cm (8 x 10 in). Extend the angle markings to the edges of the cardboard on the right half of the protractor, using a sharp pencil and a ruler.

Connect a garden hose to a faucet at one end and to a nozzle at the other end. Make sure when using the hose that no one is anywhere near your line of fire. Turn the faucet on all the way and adjust the nozzle to get as narrow a stream of water as possible. Direct the stream of water so that it is parallel to the ground.

Have a partner help you with this next step. Line up the giant protractor so that the stream of water passes alongside it and begins where the 90-degree line intersects the 0-degree line. Keep the stream of water horizontal

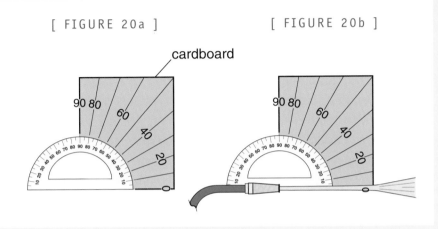

[FIGURE 20a]   [FIGURE 20b]

cardboard

90 80   90 80
60   60
40   40
20   20
0   0

20 a) You can make a giant half-protractor. b) Line up the bottom of the protractor with a stream of water directed horizontally.

and adjust the zero line vertically so that it is in line with the stream, as shown in Figure 20b. At all times, the base of the protractor should be horizontal to the ground.

Throughout the experiment, hold the nozzle so that the stream of water starts at the intersection of the 90-degree and 0-degree lines. Angle the nozzle higher and higher to get the stream to hit the ground as far away as possible. Find the launch angle.

Slow down the stream of water by reducing the flow. Again find the launch angle that yields the longest horizontal distance. How do the two angles compare?

What was the maximum angle for distance for a stream of water?

An angle of 45 degrees to the horizontal usually produces the longest distance, even when the water is slowed. The air resistance for a baseball is larger than that of the water because of the greater speed of the ball. As a result, the angle for maximum horizontal distance for a baseball in air is generally several degrees less than 45, depending on the launching speed. Tall pitchers often specialize in throwing fastballs. The extra height gives a longer arc to the pitch, which makes it harder for the batter to judge the ball's descent.

REBOUND RATING

If you have not yet obtained the rebound rating for a baseball, this is a good time to do it. Enter it into your table of rebound ratings. Baseballs are officially tested by shooting them at 85 feet per second at a wall made of wood backed by concrete. The official rebound rating is 0.32, so a baseball dropped at that speed would be expected to rebound to about one-third as high as the drop height. What did you obtain when you dropped it under the conditions you have set?

In any year with many home runs in the pro leagues, there are claims that the ball is livelier than it used to be. After 1920, baseballs were wound more tightly. This increased their rebound rating. So far, the rebound ratings of major-league baseballs have not changed since the early 1950s, when the ratings were standardized. If today's ball were to become livelier, it might result in too many home runs—which might cause many ballparks to become obsolete.

BASKETBALL

In 1891, Dr. James Naismith, a physical educator in Springfield, Massachusetts, was looking for an indoor game to be played between the football and baseball seasons. He invented basketball when he nailed a peach basket to the balcony at either end of a gymnasium and tossed in a soccer ball. That is why the game is called basketball and why the hoop assembly is called a basket.

Today, the basket is a 5/8-inch-thick ring of iron 18 inches in diameter with an open net hanging below. The basket is 15 feet from the foul line. The back of the iron rim is 6 inches from the backboard and 10 feet above the ground.

Today's basketball is large, light for its size, and bouncy. Inside the leather-covered sphere is a vulcanized rubber bladder cemented to the leather. Usually the ball is orange or brown. The cover of the basketball contains a self-sealing valve into which air is injected with a hollow needle. Most basketballs are pumped up to an air-pressure-gauge reading of between 7 and 9 pounds per square inch above the outside air pressure. Pounds per square inch is abbreviated as psi.

Basketball Measurements
20–22 oz
9.7-in diameter
0.55–0.62 rebound rating when dropped from 183 centimeters (72 inches) onto a wooden floor

Use an air pump made for use with basketballs. It will come with a pressure gauge and a needle to inject air through the self-sealing valve.

Start with 6 psi of air pressure in the basketball. How high does the ball bounce when dropped from 183 centimeters (72 inches)? Calculate the rebound rating.

Increase the air pressure to 7 psi (the lowest recommended pressure). Again measure the bounce and calculate the rebound rating.

Measure two other bounces, one at 8.5 psi and one at 9 psi (the highest recommended pressure). For each, calculate the rebound ratings.

Enter into your table the average rebound rating for a basketball in the recommended pressure range (ignore the rating for 6 psi).

How does the air pressure affect the bounce of the basketball? If the air pressure were above the recommended range, how might the game be affected?

Inside a basketball, the molecules of air are very lively, moving around, hitting one another, and pushing out the cover of the ball (see Figure 21). When the ball hits the ground and is compressed, the molecules are pushed closer together. They slap vigorously against one another and against the cover of the basketball, pushing it out again. The basketball bounces upward. When the pump increases the pressure on the basketball, it pushes more molecules of air into the same space. Now more molecules are pushing back on the cover of the basketball. They cause the ball to bounce higher.

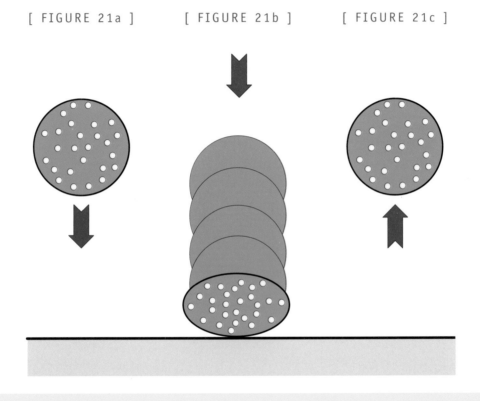

[FIGURE 21a]   [FIGURE 21b]   [FIGURE 21c]

21 a) Air particles bounce around inside a basketball. b) When the ball is compressed, the molecules bounce more often and harder. c) The ball bounces up as molecules push on all sides of the inside of the ball.

Science Fair Project Idea

How does the rebound rating of a basketball change with temperature? Measure the pressure in psi of a basketball inflated to a recommended pressure. Measure its rebound rating. Place the basketball into a refrigerator for at least eight hours. What do think will happen to the rebound rating? What do you think will happen to the pressure? Measure both immediately after removing the ball from the refrigerator. Try to explain what happened in terms of how the motion of molecules is affected by cooling. What do you predict will happen to the molecules when heated? How will this affect the rebound rating of the basketball? Test your prediction by starting with a cold basketball at 7 psi and allowing the basketball to return to room temperature. Why should an inflated basketball never be heated in a heating pad?

🏆 5.4 Topspin and Backspin

Materials:
-basketball
-smooth, level floor

Often, basketball players speed up, slow down, or turn as they dribble to pass the ball. As a result, they have to guide the direction of the ball and change its speed. Wrist, finger, and palm action are used to guide the ball. The player pushes it forward to speed it up while dribbling and pushes back to slow it down. When the ball is pushed at an angle to the floor, it rebounds up and away at the same angle (see Experiment 4.2). Through experience, the player learns the angle needed.

When the ball is bounced with spin, however, it may bounce off in some direction or at some other angle than where it had been going. A bounce pass with spin greatly reduces the chances of a steal, because it is hard to judge where the ball will go after it bounces.

Standing in place, push the ball forward toward the floor to land several feet away. Does the ball bounce off the ground at the same angle that it hit the ground? Repeat this several times to be sure.

Next, push the ball forward as before, but spin the ball downward with your fingers as you push off. You want the ball to move forward while spinning around a horizontal axis so that the top is spinning toward you. This is backspin. What happens to the ball when it bounces compared with the one with no spin?

Finally, push the ball forward but make the top spin away from you. You can do this by pushing with your palm going forward over the top of the ball. This is topspin (also called forward spin). How does the angle of the bounce compare with that of the ball bounced with no spin?

The bounce of a basketball, unlike that of a tennis ball in play (see Experiment 4.3) is quite predictable. The basketball is less affected by air friction than the tennis ball because the basketball weighs much more and its speed is low. Backspin raises the rebound angle (Figure 22a), because the spin opposes the direction of the bounce, resulting in greater ball-floor friction. The greater friction also slows the ball more than for

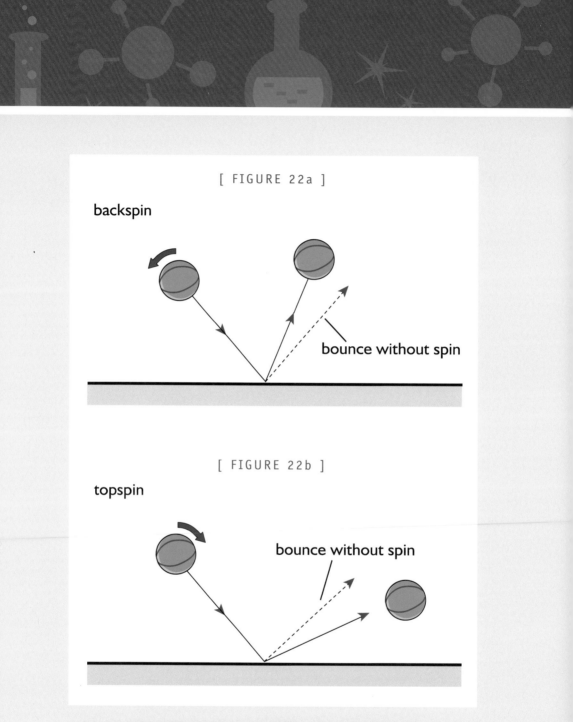

[FIGURE 22a]

backspin

bounce without spin

[FIGURE 22b]

topspin

bounce without spin

A bounce with spin results in a different rebound angle.
a) Backspin causes the rebound angle to increase.
b) Topspin (forward spin) causes the rebound angle to decrease.

the ball with no spin. Topspin lowers the rebound angle (Figure 22b), because the forward spin reduces friction as the ball rolls ahead. The ball also speeds up compared with the ball with no spin.

🏆 Science Fair Project Idea

Sidespin to the left or right can also be applied to a basketball. Find out how to spin the basketball while it is being pushed to move it left or right. Draw diagrams to illustrate the bounces. Various types of spin combinations can be used to elude opponents by making a thread-the-needle pass through the desired space.

5.5 Getting the Basketball Into the Basket

Unlike baseball, tennis, and golf, very high ball velocity is not a major factor in basketball; eye alignment and controlled velocity are important. Together with experience, they are what the player needs to get the ball into the basket. About 50 percent of attempted baskets in a major-league game land in the basket. Foul shots go in about 90 percent of the time.

Practice throwing the ball into the basket on a dribble as you run from one side of the court to the other. On the throw, should you aim the ball directly at the hoop? Or where? Why? If you aim at the basket, the ball will miss it. Recall that when you are dribbling the ball, it is moving in the same direction that you are. So, in the same way, when you shoot a ball while you are running, the ball will have the forward motion from your run and the sideways motion from your throw. The ball should be aimed toward the basket but a little in back of where you want it to end up.

A helicopter or airplane making a pass over a field to drop provisions to hungry people or to soldiers must use the same principle. If the packet is dropped directly over the target, it will miss it completely. The motion given to the packet by the fast-moving airplane has to be considered. Similarly, a parachutist who jumps out of the plane is still moving forward as the plane was and, to be safe, must wait until he has descended well below the airplane before opening the chute.

Materials:
- basketball
- hoop
- weights
- 2 chairs
- straight metal rod (optional)

What is the best way to get the ball into the basket, to carom it off the backboard or to send it directly through the hoop? Most coaches feel that front shots (including free shots) and distant shots should be thrown directly into the basket. Also, the one-handed jump shot made close to the basket should be tossed directly through the rim. Other shots are bounced off the backboard. The most common shot today is a jump shot launched one-handed in midair.

Is spin ever helpful in landing the ball in the basket?

To observe this, an expert player is needed who can throw the ball with spin onto the front or back rim of the basket. Then you can observe it from below.

Without an expert player, one solution is to lower a hoop so that you can toss and observe it at the same time. You can use the seats of two chairs on either side of the hoop to hold it so that the basketball can go through the hoop; bricks or other heavy objects on either side can hold the hoop firmly in place. A straight metal rod of the same diameter as the hoop rod can be substituted; it needs to be firmly pinned down, too. Toss the basketball with different spins onto the front and onto the back rims of the hoop or onto the rod near the top. How can you use spin to help the ball get into the basket? What did you do? Why does it work?

Backspin is one of the important elements in the scientific formula for helping the ball into the basket. A "friendly roll" may occur when a shot with backspin bounces on the rim before going in. The backspin causes the ball to bounce off the rim with a decrease in forward speed. As a result, a ball that could otherwise bounce away might roll into the basket.

FOOTBALL

A ball that is very different from the balls examined so far is the football. For one thing, it is far from spherical. Moreover, it is not only thrown or carried in a game but also kicked. It is never intentionally bounced during a game.

The modern game of football originated during a soccer game. It started in 1823 when a player at Rugby College was having trouble kicking a ball. He picked it up and ran across the entire field to make a "touchdown." He got into trouble, but the fans loved it. The game quickly became popular. In the 1880s, Walter Camp invented the set scrimmage. Amos Alonzo Stagg invented the T formation in 1890. The pass was not used until 1913, when Knute Rockne and Gus Dorais used it to beat West Point in an electrifying game.

The shape of a football is spheroidal (roundish but not spherical). The modern ball is covered by four panels sewn together. A rubber bladder inside the cover is blown up to 12.5–13.5 pounds of air pressure

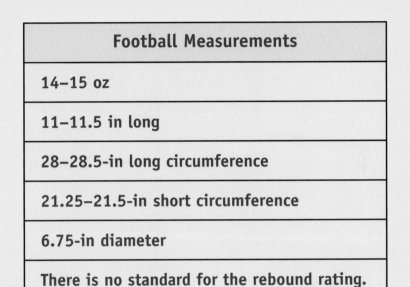

Football Measurements
14–15 oz
11–11.5 in long
28–28.5-in long circumference
21.25–21.5-in short circumference
6.75-in diameter
There is no standard for the rebound rating.

per square inch. The opening is then neatly laced together with sturdy laces. A football is easy to conceal under the arm while running.

AIR DRAG ON A FOOTBALL

The tapered ends of a football give it a streamlined shape. Its long back fills the space that would otherwise have been occupied by the wake. A wake is the disturbed region behind an object when it moves through a fluid. For example, a boat that moves through water leaves a wake of rough water behind it. Air behaves like a fluid. When the football moves through it, the tapered back of the football produces a narrowed wake with reduced drag. The drag is less than that of a round ball of similar volume, such as a soccer ball. The shape of the football was adopted because of such advantages in flight.

The bounce of a football is erratic and clumsy looking. Yet when a football goes spiraling through the air in a huge arc that slices between the goal posts, it is a thing of beauty.

5.1 The Football Is an Odd Ball

Materials:
- football
- measuring tape

You can learn a lot about a football by bouncing it.

Drop a football from shoulder height so that it falls tapered-end down (nose down). Repeat several times. What happens?

Now drop the football broadside (onto the widest part). To do this, hold the football between your hands by the tapered ends, laces up. Release it so that it falls straight down. Compare with the nose-down drop.

Determine the rebound ratings for the football when dropped onto its nose and when dropped broadside.

Was there a difference in the two rebound ratings? Why do you think this is?

Does a football bounce higher than a baseball? A tennis ball? Does it make any difference how it is dropped?

A football dropped nose down usually makes a low bounce to one side. This is because the nose collapses unevenly. As the ball pushes back into shape, the ball is off center, tilts, and falls over.

When the football is dropped broadside, it falls on a wide area compared to the little nose. That area is pressed smoothly inward and the ball smoothly resumes shape. As a result, the ball is pushed straight up. This bounce is higher than that of a baseball and in the same range as that of a tennis ball.

Is the flight of a football in air different from that of the more spherical balls that have been observed so far?

Throw a rubber ball as far as you can and observe where it hits the ground.

Toss a football forward the way you did the rubber ball, but heave the football from the tapered end. Be sure that it has no spin. Repeat a few times. Can you get it to go about as far as the rubber ball or is the flight much shorter?

Hold the football with your palm over the laces. Throw it so that it travels with a tapered end at each side. How does this compare with nose-first flight and to the rubber ball's flight? Which way did it go the farthest? The least far?

Neither throw gets the football as far as the rubber ball. A football without spin is called a floater. Any little wind or twist can cause its nose to tilt down and dive. In the above activity, the nose-first throw may have gone slightly farther than the broadside throw. The broad side of the football exposes more surface as it surges through the air, so it develops more drag.

Now throw a football so that it spins around its long axis; see Figure 23. The long axis extends from nose to nose. Experts advise that this throw be done by holding the ball so that the flesh pads at the tips of your fingers are at the laces. Bring the ball back and then throw it forward with a flick of the wrist and a push of the index finger. How does the distance traveled compare with that of the same throw without spin?

What happens when you throw a football with spin, broadside first?

Throw a football so that the tapered ends rotate end over end. How did you get the ball to do it? How did the ball move?

The spinning football goes much farther than without spin in all of the throws in this activity. The longest flight occurs when the ball is thrown with spin around the long axis, because that throw produces the least drag (exposes the least surface as the ball bores through the air).

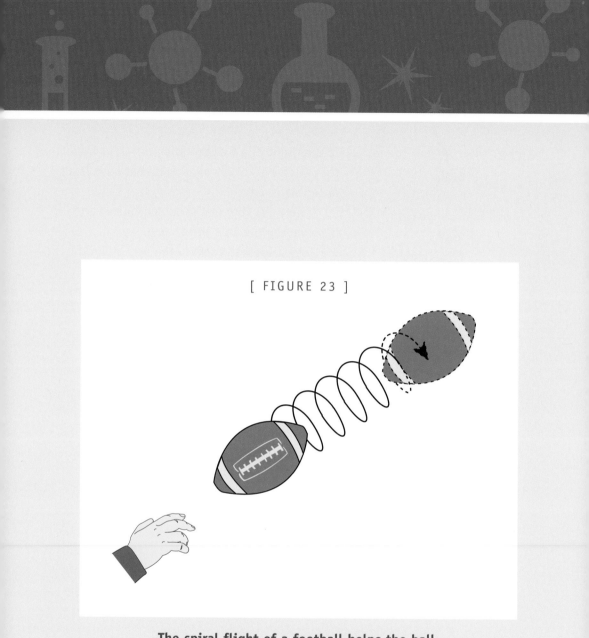

[FIGURE 23]

The spiral flight of a football helps the ball travel farther than without spin.

Science Fair Project Idea

When a spinning ball is thrown with the tapered ends at either side, does it have forward spin or backspin? Is there a Magnus force acting on it (see Chapter 3)? Assemble several friends and have them heave the football (tapered ends to the side) as far as they can with spin and without. Measure the greatest distance for each throw and then average the throws with and without spin. What do you conclude?

🏆 5.9 Punting a Football

A football may be punted or place kicked. A punter drops the ball toward his foot and kicks it before it reaches the ground (see Figure 24). Punting can occur during the fourth down of a football game. The offense punts the ball after it has tried unsuccessfully to move upfield. The punter needs to be concerned about three things: angle of launch, tightness of the spiral, and air conditions.

The punter always wants the ball to fly nose first in a spiral. The kick is made at the top of the foot between the toe and ankle. When kicking with the right leg, the player obtains the spiral by a kick that goes from right to left across the bottom of the ball.

Try punting the ball yourself or ask an expert to do it. The punter should be wearing football shoes. Practice on a football field or other wide-open space with no one else within range of the ball.

Drop the ball from as high as possible and punt it. What effect does this have compared with a lower drop? Why is this technique not used during a game? What happens when you lower the drop to hip height and try to kick it?

The punter wants the ball to go as far as possible and to have as long a hang time (time in flight) as possible. The long hang time allows the team to get down the field to tackle the receiver. Unfortunately, hang time and horizontal distance oppose each other. The higher the angle of the punt, the less the distance. As with other balls, a 45-degree angle of launch gives the most distance, but the punter usually kicks it at 50 degrees to get more hang time.

Hang time and distance are controlled by varying the angle of the kicking foot and the height from the ground at which the ball is kicked. Punters drop the football with the laces up because the lace area is the least elastic part of the ball.

[FIGURE 24]

A punter kicks the ball so that its nose travels first.

Winds are the worst enemy of the punter because they cause the ball to veer. Based on experience, the punter must consider and adjust to how the winds will affect the flight of the ball.

Science Fair Project Idea

How does the angle of a kick affect the hang time and the ground distance? Try kicking the ball at three different angles; this may take considerable practice. Make one as high as you can manage, one from a lower angle that still allows the ball to go far, and one in between. Take measurements of the hang time and of the horizontal distance that the ball goes before it hits the ground. What do you conclude about the relationship between angle and hang time, between hang time and distance, and between angle and distance?

Appendix 1:
Ball Sizes and Rebound Ratings

The rebound ratings in this table are those set up by the recognized professional associations for competitions. Where no requirement has been set, "no standard" is written in the table and the rating given was determined by accelerating a new ball under the stated conditions.

Ball	Weight (oz)	Diameter (in)	Rebound rating	Measurement conditions
Baseball	5–5.25	2.9	0.32	Fired at 85 ft/sec at a wall of ash boards backed by concrete
Basketball	20–22	9.7	0.55–0.62	Dropped from 72 inches onto a wooden floor
Football	14–15	Length: 11–11.5 Long circumference 28–28.5; short circumference 21.25–21.5 with diameter about 6.75	No standard	
Golf ball	1.62	U.S.: 1.68; British: 1.62	0.89 (no standard)	Dropped from 60 inches onto ceramic tile
Rubber ball	3.5–4	2.5	0.33–0.58 (no standard)	Dropped from 60 inches onto ceramic tile
Tennis ball	>2.00–<2.06	>2.5–<2.625	>0.53–<0.58	Dropped from 100 inches onto concrete

Several Superballs were tested and found to have an average rebound rating of 0.88 when dropped from 60 inches onto a tile floor.

The rebound rating is the distance a ball rebounds divided by the distance from which it is dropped or fired (length of rebound divided by length of drop). See Experiment 3.3 for a discussion. Since the rebound rating depends on both the ball and the surface onto which it is dropped, the flooring or wall must always be described with the rating.

If a rubber ball dropped from a height of 80 inches onto an asphalt floor rebounds to a height of 45 inches, its rebound rating is

$$\frac{45 \text{ in}}{80 \text{ in}} = 0.56$$

This shows that the ball bounced back from an asphalt floor up to a height that was 56/100 (0.56 or 56 percent) of its starting height of 80 inches. The same rebound rating is obtained when you measure the distances in the metric system.

FURTHER READING

Books

Bochinski, Julianne Blair. *The Complete Workbook for Science Fair Projects.* Hoboken, N.J.: John Wiley and Sons, Inc., 2005.

Gifford, Clive. *Soccer: The Ultimate Guide to the Beautiful Game.* New York: Kingfisher Publications, Inc., 2002.

Levine, Shar and Leslie Johnstone. *Sport Science.* New York: Sterling Publishing Co., Inc., 2006.

Moorman, Thomas. *How to Make Your Science Project Scientific.* Revised Edition. New York: John Wiley & Sons, Inc., 2002.

Ominsky, David and P. J. Harari. *Football Made Simple: A Spectator's Guide.* Los Angeles, Calif.: First Base Sports, Inc., 2006.

Pentland, Peter and Pennie Stoyles. *Toy and Game Science.* Broomall, Pa.: Chelsea House Publishers, 2003.

Wiese, Jim, and Ed Shems. *Sports Science: 40 Goal-Scoring, High-Flying, Medal-Winning Experiments for Kids.* N.Y.: John Wiley, 2002.

Internet Addresses

Kenneth Lafferty Hess Family Charitable Foundation. *Science Buddies.* 2002–2008. <http://www.sciencebuddies.org/>.

Science Hound. *All Science Fair Projects.com.* 2006. <http://all-science-fair-projects.com/>.

The President's Challenge. *The President's Challenge Physical Activity and Fitness Awards Program.* <http://www.presidentschallenge.org/>.

INDEX